9
family
day care

Edited by
Carol Seefeldt, Ph.D.
and
Laura L. Dittmann, Ph.D.

☆ U.S. GOVERNMENT PRINTING OFFICE : 1975   O—508—105

For sale by the Superintendent of Documents, U.S. Government Printing Office,
Washington, D.C. 20402 - Price: $1.90
Stock Number 1791—00188

foreword

It is estimated that over 91 percent of all day care services in the United States takes place in private home settings commonly referred to as "Family Day Care Homes." The focus of this handbook is to consider the distinguishing characteristics, variations, advantages and disadvantages of this type of child care services for all children needing such services.

The information is intended to be of interest and help to the person who is thinking about starting a family day care program, the individual who already is offering such services, and agencies which may be thinking of coordinating a network of family day care homes. The first part of the handbook is especially intended for parents who are trying to decide which type of day care arrangement would be best for their child. Should it be day care in their own home? In someone else's home? Or in a day care center?

Whatever the child's age, the length of time each day he or she will be in someone else's care, and whatever the setting, day care services should be selected with great care to ensure the best possible environment for the nurturing, learning and protection of the child.

The addition of this handbook to the Office of Child Development's day care series will further increase the wide range of information regarding day care services for children of various ages with various needs.

acknowledgments

This Manual, designed to serve three major audiences—the family seeking day care for its children, the family desiring to begin a family day care service, and the agency considering implementing a family day care system—has been the result of the effort of many individuals. We would like to thank the following persons who served as the review panel for the initial drafts of the Manual and provided valuable advice.

Diane Bray, Family Day Care Mother, Rockville, Maryland

Virginia Burke, National Institutes of Health, DHEW

Madeline G. Dowling, Community Services Administration, SRS, DHEW

Edna Gigax, Family Day Care Mother, Washington, D.C.

Alice Gilliam, Family Day Care Mother, Baltimore, Maryland

Marjorie Grosett, Day Care Council of New York

Gertrude Hoffman, Community Services Administration, SRS, DHEW

Carolyn Hoolahan, Montgomery County Department of Social Services, Maryland

Barbara Johnson, New York State Department of Social Services

Anna A. Keene, Family Day Care Mother, Baltimore, Maryland

Deria Moore, Home Start Program, Office of Child Development, DHEW

Thomas Piscitelli, Department of Social Services, Baltimore, Maryland

Mary Bea Preston, Maryland 4-C Staff, Baltimore, Maryland

Peggy Restivo, Family Day Care Mother, Baltimore, Maryland

Charles Root, New York State Department of Social Services

June S. Sale, Pacific Oaks College, Pasadena, California

Florence Seguin, Home Start Program, Office of Child Development, DHEW

A special appreciation is extended to those persons who provided material for the Manual.

1. Cynthia Bell, University of Maryland, College Park, Maryland
2. Estelle Brook, Department of Social Services, Jacksonville, Florida
3. Madeline G. Dowling, Community Services Administration, SRS, DHEW
4. Mattie Feldman, New York, New York
5. Richard Feldman, Bank Street College, New York, New York
6. Marjorie Grosett, Day Care Council of New York, New York, New York
7. Carolyn Hoolahan, Montgomery County Department of Social Services, Rockville, Maryland
8. Mary Jackson, Assistant Director, New York Family Day Care Program, New York, New York
9. Lois Barclay Murphy, Washington, D.C.

The final review panel, Sister Mary Mal O'Dowd, Gwen Morgan, Sam Granato, Gertrude Hoffman, and Edna Hughes, offered valuable assistance in shaping the contents of the Manual.

Barbara Ruffino
Project Director/Associate Editor
Kirschner Associates, Inc.

contents

introduction

WHAT IS FAMILY DAY CARE?

Some mothers and fathers are not able to be at home during the day to care for their children. Formerly, the child's grandmother, aunt or neighbor would help the family by caring for the child. More and more these days, the grandmothers and aunts either live too far away, or go to work themselves, and cannot take on the task. A family must find someone else to care for its children for part of the day.

There are several different types of care a mother and father may choose for their child —they might select a day care center program where many children are cared for together in one place, they might ask someone to come into their home and care for the children there, they might decide that a family day care home will be best for their child, or they may decide on a combination of these day care services.

Family day care is the care of a child in the home of another family. Usually there are no more than six children in the home, and some of these children may be the caregiver's. Family day care is closest to the child's experience in his own family—or it should be—because a child, whether he is a tiny baby, a preschooler or a preteen, goes to another home, and has the opportunity to form a continuous relationship through the day with the family day care mother and father.

Family day care is a good plan for many families:

Infants and very young children may be well served in a quality family day care home. Very young children have little experience relating to other people. In a family day care home there are only a few other children and adults with whom to relate and the young child will not be overwhelmed by a large number of children or staff.

Preschool children may also find a good family day care home suited to their needs. In a family day care home they may receive the personal attention they need. Here too, the preschool child has the opportunity to learn to get along with a few others—both younger and older than himself. He may also find a degree of flexibility suited to his needs in the home, with the opportunity to eat, rest, and play when he chooses.

Children who are emotionally troubled, physically handicapped, or mentally retarded may be comfortable and happy in the small, flexible setting of a family day care home. Some children with handicaps find they can learn and develop at their own pace in the family day care home with the patient support and personal encouragement of a trained, sensitive caregiver.

School age children are often very comfortable in a family day care home. It gives them a place to go before or after school while their parents are away. Here they can stay in their own neighborhood and lead much the same kind of life they would at home. They may even have the companionship of their brothers and sisters. They are free to go to the homes of their friends, or have their friends over to the family day care home. The school age child can take part in after school activities or sports, and even join an organized neighborhood group—a crafts club, or Girl or Boy Scouts.

For children who find it interesting or exciting to be around children of different ages, rather than all children of their own age, family day care may be a good choice. For some children there is a special challenge in the activities of older children. Some children are benefited by having older children as a needed model, a 'big brother'' or "big sister." This may be particularly important for "only" children or children from one parent families.

In sparsely populated areas where centers are far from the homes of the parents, or where the population does not justify a center program, a family day care home may be within easy reach.

For parents who work odd hours, when centers are not usually open, a family day care home may be a wise choice. The home might take care of the children of parents who must work late at night, or even on weekends.

Families with several children often find a family day care home convenient. Here the baby, the preschooler, and the school age child may be cared for together, and the need to find a different program for each child is eliminated. Having an older brother or younger sister around is a comforting feeling for a child who spends part of his day away from home. Often too, the caregiver adjusts her fee when several children from the same family are being cared for in the home.

Parents may have more choice in the selection of the person who is going to care for their child. They are free to select persons as caregivers for the children whom they feel have similar ideas on raising children, or have similar values. This may make the adjustment easier for the child, since they might be in a setting where the environment and attitudes are the same as in their own home.

Flexible arrangements may also be possible in a family day care home. A family may wish to take advantage of a Head Start program in their area, or enroll their child in a church or private nursery school with a half-day program. The caregiver may take the child to the nursery school or Head Start center, and pick him up later, or the home may have a cooperative arrangement with a nursery school or child development center. Parents are then able to plan for a wide variety of experiences for their children.

WHAT DOES A FAMILY DAY CARE HOME OFFER?

A "home away from home," a quality family day care home offers to the children all of the nurturing love and attention, and all the experiences in family living they would have in their own home. Informal in nature, daily activities in a good day care home are carefully planned to give each individual child the type of care

and experiences he needs to grow emotionally, socially, physically, and intellectually. These activities give each child the opportunity to:

- participate in usual household routines
- live with both younger and older children
- do the same things and use the same community resources as others of his age in the neighborhood
- be himself—to feel angry, shy or happy— to eat what he likes, to rest and play when he needs to
- feel comfortable and confident in himself, in the safety and security of a home
- have his basic needs fulfilled, helping him to grow socially, emotionally, physically, and intellectually

A Quality Family Day Care Home Offers

learning activities

"The entire home is an environment for learning. In the kitchen the child learns how to dismantle and reassemble a metal coffee pot, or how to stack the multitude of pots and pans found on the bottom shelf. In the bathroom he learns to wash his hands as soon as he can climb onto a stool and turn the faucet on without scalding himself."*

In the ideal family day care home, learning takes place everywhere, all day long. Here there is time for the children to play, to explore and experiment with their environment, both in the home and the neighborhood. All of the experiences the children have in a good family day care home help them to learn more about themselves, others and the world about them.

In the home the children:

learn about health and safety

Children experience healthful living as they brush their teeth after eating, or wash their hands before eating. The daily routines of playing, resting, eating, washing and dressing, that happen in the same order each day, help the children to develop attitudes and skills necessary to living a healthy, safe life.

---

*Sale, J., *Open the Door—See the People,* Pacific Oaks College, Pasadena, California, 1972.

learn as they play

Everyday in a well organized day care home there is plenty of time for both in and outdoor play. Children play by themselves, or with others, they play with crayon and paper, with dress up clothes, or with puzzles and peg boards. Outside, children can play more actively—they run, climb, jump, and swing. As they play they learn how to cooperate, how to do things, and how things in their world work.

learn to use language

Language can't be separated from any other activity in a good home. As the children play, they talk. A walk around the neighborhood is filled with language. Everything the children do—playing, cooking, digging in the sand, gives them something else to talk about, something else to tell their mothers and fathers, some other experience to put words to. Every day, maybe several times a day, the caregiver reads a story or poem to the children and plays some music or records for them, or listens as the school age child reads to her.

learn about the world around them

Walks to the park, store, or playground, and all of the people who come and go from the home—neighbors, mailmen, repairmen—give children knowledge about their world. Children, watching and helping the caregiver prepare meals, are finding out about food—where it comes from, how it changes as it cooks, bakes, or freezes. Planting the seeds from the apple they just ate or taking a walk in the new fallen snow teaches the children about their world.

learn to be creative

All people are creative, and children in a family day care home have the time and opportunity to use crayons, paste, scissors, and all kinds of boxes and scrap materials to create with and give expression to their ideas and feelings.

A Quality Family Day Care Home Offers

a caregiving person

More important than the activities offered in the family day care home is the caregiver. He or she is the one who becomes "like a parent" to the children. He or she holds and cuddles the baby, singing him to sleep, and listens and talks to the preschooler, laughing at his

"jokes." The caregiver gives the school age child the security and supervised freedom he needs to explore his neighborhood, and the support he needs to succeed in school. The caregiver offers many of the things a mother or father would. The caregiver:

- comforts the hurt or frightened child.
- shows he or she cares for each child, admiring his drawings, taking the time to tell his parents how much he enjoyed his day, showing them that he respects and values both them and their child.
- understands when the child feels angry, frustrated, or hateful and helps him to talk out his feelings, to work through them without making him feel less than he should about himself for having strong feelings.
- is aware of differences in children, and provides for these differences—finding a dark, quiet place for Manuel who needs this to nap, and a game for Susan, who does not nap, but needs to rest, to play quietly by herself.

A Quality Family Day Care Home Offers

other people

A good family day care home offers the children the chance to learn to live with others, in a family-like environment. In a family day care home the children can:

- live with their own brothers and sisters, both younger and older than they;
- be like a family with the caregiver's children, husband, wife, mother, or father;
- learn what older people are like if a grandmother or grandfather lives in at home;
- have a substitute father when the caregiver's husband plays with the children, picks them up for a hug when he comes home, or helps the older ones to repair a bike or build a fort;
- learn to play and work with new friends and others in the neighborhood.

All good day care, whether it is a center program or care of the child in a home, should offer the children the opportunity to learn about others, the world around them, and to relate to a sensitive, mothering person. Family day care is unique in that it offers the children this care on a smaller scale, and it gives the parents one more choice in selecting the very best day care arrangement for their families and children.

section
I

chapter 1

What Parents Should Look For in Selecting a Family Day Care Home For Their Children

FINDING A FAMILY DAY CARE HOME

Having made the decision to place your child in a family day care home, you will want to carefully select a home, similar to your own, that will give your child the type of care and activities you yourself would provide.

The Department of Social Services in your community is often a good source of information for helping you to find a family day care home. A local planning council, religious organization, Head Start center, or neighborhood day care center or school may also be able to help you find a home suited to your needs.

Some family day care homes are part of a "system" or group of homes operated by an agency, school or child development center. These homes are usually licensed or approved by the sponsoring group and supervised by them. If the home you are considering is affiliated with a system of homes, find out how much supervision is given the home and what the agency requirements and standards are. It may be that this home is well qualified to offer quality family day care for your child.

In some areas of the country, family day care homes must be licensed. A license will protect you and your child. If a license is required in your state, ask to see the licensing requirements. Do these requirements represent the kind of quality you are looking for? Check for yourself whether the home meets the requirements, since it is not always possible for state licensing agencies to make frequent inspections.

Visit several homes, trying to find some that are located close to your own home so that transportation will not be difficult and the children will stay in their own neighborhood, among people and things they know. As you visit the homes, look for the following things:

The Home Itself

Children can be cared for anywhere, however, you will want to be certain that the condition of the home is safe for children.

As you visit the home, ask yourself:

- Is there a space for the children to play inside?
- Is there a space for the children to play outside? Is it fenced? Away from traffic or other danger?
- Are the rooms well lighted, safe and in good repair?
- Is there adequate heating and ventilation?
- Where will the children rest? Does each child have his own cot? Is there enough space for all of the children to rest?
- Is there some space for them to keep their own things?
- Is the kitchen clean, and are all appliances working?
- Is the bathroom safe for children? Are there footstools for the children to reach the faucets and toilet? Are these in good working order?
- If there are stairs, are they guarded and do they have a handrail?
- Is there a place to keep a child who becomes ill?
- Are there books for the children to read, or the mother to read to the children?
- Is there someplace for the school age child to study?
- Is there a workable fire extinguisher available?
- Are emergency numbers posted near the telephone?
- Are the walls free of lead paint?

The Activities in the Home

The daily activities in the family day care home

are informal, so your child will have the opportunity to benefit from experiences of family living. As you visit the home, ask the caregiver about the activities she plans for the children. Ask her:

- Will there be time for indoor and outdoor play?
- Can the children take part in the activities of the community—the YMCA, Brownies, Girl or Boy Scouts, Boys' Clubs, or other organized groups?
- Are routines—snacks, meals, rest—planned for at regular times?
- Will the child be able to draw, paint, color, and make things with his hands?
- Will there be music for him to listen to?
- Will the mother read a story to the children every day?
- Will the mother take the children on walks around the neighborhood?
- Can the children take part in the household activities—helping to prepare food, picking up their toys, and taking care of their own things?
- Will the mother teach the children the same things you would in your own home?

The Family Day Care Mother or Father

Although the condition of the home and the activities planned are very important to you and your children, they may not be as important as the caregiver. The person who will be caring for the children, who will be taking your place, is the most important factor in the family day care home. You will want him or her to be very much like yourself, caring for and loving your children in the same way you would. As you talk with the mother or father, ask yourself:

- How does she or he feel about me?
- Does the caregiver really like children?
- Is she or he calm, do they have a sense of humor, are they kind?
- Does the caregiver listen when children talk to him or her, and answer their questions patiently?
- Do the children in the home seem to like the caregiver?
- Do the children seem happy? Are they able to express unhappiness and anger and get comfort and help from the caregiver?
- Even so, does the caregiver control the children, remaining clearly in charge, kindly and firmly?

- Does the caregiver let the children make suggestions and do things themselves?
- Is the caregiver so neat and clean that the children could not play freely in the home?
- Does the caregiver show you that she or he understands each child and meets the needs of each of the children?
- Do you think the caregiver can deal with problems as they come up?
- How do you think he or she would act in an emergency?
- Will the caregiver take the time to maintain relations with you, and not try to take over your place in your children's lives?
- Does she or he have the health and energy to take care of children?

Others in the Home

Often, the other people in the family day care home can influence the kind of experience your children will have. One person cannot care for many children at the same time. Ask yourself:

- How many children are already in the home?
- How does the mother take care of her own children? How many does she have?
- Are there younger children in the home? Older children?
- How will they feel about your children?
- What about the caregiver's family? Will her older children or husband object to her taking care of your children?
- Are there invalids, or others demanding a great deal of care in the home?
- What is the procession of others in the home—ask specifically who will be coming and going from the home—college age children, teenagers, elderly relatives?

Health and Safety

The physical condition of the home will help you to decide if the home is safe for children. However, there are other things you might ask about:

- Are the windows screened and locked?
- How are the meals planned? Will there be a mid-morning and afternoon snack in addition to a hot lunch?
- What is the plan for emergencies and accidents? Do the children practice an emergency plan?
- Is the caregiver aware of the dangers of giving medicines, even aspirin and cough

syrups, to children without permission?
- Are poisons and household cleaners locked and out of reach of the children?
- Does the caregiver practice good health habits—teaching the children to wash their hands, brush their teeth, etc.? And does she or he have proof of a recent physical examination showing that she or he is free from TB, etc.?

Reaching Agreement

Having found a home where you think your child would be happy and well cared for, you will want to reach agreement with the caregiver on several things. If you and she do things too much differently, your children may not be content and comfortable. If there is too much difference between you and the caregiver, the children may become upset. Talk over with the caregiver such things as:
- discipline—find out her ideas on discipline and punishment
- toilet training—be certain you agree on how the child will be taught
- feeding and eating patterns—these should be similar to your own
- be certain you agree on the types of activities the children can do—such as go to the playground after school, or take walks in the neighborhood, or even go for rides in the caregiver's car
- business details—how much the fee will be, when it is due, how many hours your child will be in the home, and what will happen during vacations or emergencies, and so on

If Your Choice is a Mistake

If, after several weeks, the way your child acts tells you that he is happy about going to the family day care home, then you will know you have chosen wisely. If your child is getting along fine in the home, he will:
- talk about the things he did during the day
- talk about the caregiver, what she does and says
- be eager and happy to go to the home in the morning, and just as happy to return to his own home in the evenings
- be active and cheerful
- continue in his same eating, sleeping patterns
- be eager to learn new things and go new places

It's natural for a child to cry when he's been left. He may be worried that his mother or father is not coming back, or he may be expressing his unhappiness over having to leave his own home. However, if your child:
- cries when you take him to the home
- becomes afraid to let you out of his sight
- starts sucking his thumb, wetting in the bed, or pulling at his hair, or in other ways tells you he is tense
- appears listless, refuses to eat, is afraid to sleep

then you may want to check to see if the home you have chosen is the best for you and the child. First talk to the caregiver to see if she or he knows what is troubling the child. Or you might contact the agency to see if there is someone with whom you can talk with and could help you. You and the caregiver should not be embarrassed if the home is not the right place for your child. The caregiver and you should understand that not every place, no matter how good the care is, can meet the needs of every child.

Summary

Before you make the final decision about placing your child in a family day care home be sure that you are at least satisfied that:
- you and your child have visited the home at least once while other children are there;
- you like the way the day care mother works with the other children in the home and how she will work with yours;
- your child will feel welcome in the home by the other children or anyone else living in the home;
- the day care mother has a good idea of what she will do with the children during the day, that she has routines which include rest, meals, snacks and play planned for at regular times;
- the house is safe and comfortable for children—that there are not too many "breakables" around or sharp edges and that there is good light;
- there are enough exits for the children if an emergency arises and that the children are able to practice what they should do in an emergency;
- there are no other people in the home, or likely to visit it, whom you would not like around your children.

chapter 2

The Responsibilities of Parents in the Family Day Care System

YOUR RESPONSIBILITIES

You and the family day care mother or father must work hand-in-hand to give your child the best possible care. In a way, you and the caregiver depend on one another to give the children the best experiences possible. Even though your life is very busy, and you have the care of your own household, you will have to share with the caregiver some of the responsibilities of a family day care home.

Your responsibilities might include:

Sharing Information

The family day care mother or father will need to know all about your child and your family in order to provide for him in a way that meets his needs. Be willing and ready to give this information in writing to the caregiver:

- phone numbers and addresses of your places of work, your relatives or friends that might be contacted in an emergency, phone numbers of your doctors, and the hospital you will choose if needed.
- medical information on your child. In signed writing, give permission for the caregiver to call the child's doctor in an emergency or allow emergency treatment to be given if you are not available.
- your child's eating and sleeping patterns, how he likes to spend his day, what he enjoys and does not enjoy doing. Tell the caregiver the words your family uses to describe elimination, and how the child lets you know he needs to use the bathroom. You might tell how you handle minor problems—homework, certain friends or language with the school age children.
- tell her about the clubs your school age child will be going to, and a list of names, phone numbers, and addresses of the friends your children may play with.
- let the caregiver know about other situations the child has been in—such as a center program, Sunday school, or previous day care home.

Preparing Your Child

It is part of your responsibility to prepare your child to go to someone else's home. You might, if he is old enough, talk over some of the reasons for placing him in a home, and tell him some of the things he should expect.

- visit the home with the child before you have to leave him there
- tell him what he will be doing . . . "You will eat lunch with Mrs. B.," "you will take a nap." Do not tell the child anything which is not true; this makes it harder for him, not easier.
- have him select some favorite toy or object from home to take with him the first days
- let him know where you will be during the day. You might take him to work with you one day, so he has some idea of what you will be doing while he is at the family day care home.
- tell him exactly when you will return for him. If he can't tell time, tell him, "I will pick you up after your nap," or "when the street light turns on."
- when your child is of school age, be certain he knows who he will be allowed to play with, and what after school activities he can participate in

And when it is time for the child to leave the day care home, perhaps because he has outgrown the need or your work plans have changed, prepare him for this change also. Let him know ahead of time the reason he will no longer be going to the home. Help him make the good-bye's easier. You can plan a good-bye party, let him visit in the home occasionally, or keep in touch with the caregiver with notes or phone calls.

Business Arrangements

Remember the family day care mother or father is running a business. She or he will want to be treated as you would like your employer to treat you. Just as you have regular hours and pay, the caregiver should also have regular hours and pay. Be certain to agree on the amount you will pay, when the fee will be due, and what the fee includes. If you have to leave the child in her care for a longer time than agreed upon, you will expect to pay her for extra services.

It may be that you will have questions or complaints about the caregiver. Talk directly to the caregiver about your concerns rather than telling or complaining to your children, friends, or neighbors. If you learn to go to her with your questions, or problems, you will find that you learn to understand one another, and you will begin to establish a working relationship. Even though you and the caregiver will probably become very close friends, the caregiver cannot and should not be asked to handle your personal problems.

Communicate Often

Take a few moments to talk to the caregiver in the morning and evening as you bring the children and pick them up. Even though your days are rushed and you are hoping to be on time for work in the mornings and anxious to return home to fix dinner in the evenings, allow some time to talk with your child's caregiver. Tell her the little things she needs to know about your child —the cold he seems to be coming down with, how much he enjoyed baking bread, or ask her how the day went and what your child did.

Call the caregiver in the evening occasionally to discuss your plans for your children, or just to ask her if you can help her with anything, or provide any materials—such as paper bags for drawing, or some toys.

If you have some time off, an hour in the afternoon or a lunch hour, ask the day care mother or father if you can visit with her or him and your children in the home. You can watch your children getting along with others, and can better understand the things the caregiver is trying to do with the children.

You could invite the caregiver and his or her family to some special activity in your home, such as a birthday party for your child, or a special thank you dinner or picnic.

Once in a while the caregiver may ask you to spend a few minutes, in a more formal way, to discuss your child and his progress, and plan for his future. The time you spend together in this way is important to you and your child. Use this time to review your child's medical records, keeping the caregiver up-to-date on anything new that the doctor has told you and any changes in telephone numbers and emergency procedures. As children grow and develop, their needs change. You will want to talk about changing sleeping and eating patterns, or your child's increasing needs to visit places in the neighborhood and to do things such as going to the library. Discuss your plans for the future with the caregiver. If, after the child goes to school or reaches a certain age, you will no longer require the caregiver's services, make plans with her ahead of time.

Participating in the Activities of the Home

Your child will feel your concern for him, and your interest in his daily activities if you can share in some of the responsibilities of the family day care home:

- participate in some of the activities. Perhaps on the child's birthday you might bring a cake to the home, or help to celebrate some other special event.
- you might bring some of your children's favorite books to the home, or pick up books from the library to take to the home.
- volunteer to repaint or repair damaged toys or equipment.
- help to build outdoor play equipment.

Meeting With Other Parents

If your family day care home is a part of a system of homes under an agency, there may be times when the social service agency arranges for meetings of parents. They may plan special programs about things you can do with your children, or other topics that might be of interest to you. Be ready to participate in some of these meetings.

Policy Councils

When your home is one of a system under a social service agency, you may be asked to serve on the Policy Council or the Board of Directors of the agency. The Policy Council is responsible for establishing the policies for the family day care homes. Parents are often asked to become members of this board, or asked to attend meetings, so they can participate in making decisions that will affect their children's welfare.

section
II

chapter 1

Practical Considerations Before Offering Family Day Care in Your Home

There are many reasons for persons to want to offer day care in their home. Some find that caring for other children is a good way to provide playmates and companionship for their own children. Some need to add to their income without having to work outside of the home; others may have started by offering to care for the child of a neighbor. Many others enter family day care because they truly enjoy the laughter and excitement that children bring to their home.

Whatever your reasons, if you respect, understand and enjoy children, and know how to provide for their growth and development, you will probably be able to succeed as a family day care mother. More than likely, you will enjoy your experience. But before you decide to offer day care for children in your home there are some practical things which you should consider very seriously. If you are aware of these factors, before you begin to offer day care, the chances that you will enjoy your venture will be greater.

YOUR FAMILY

As the words 'family day care' indicate, caring for children in your home involves the entire family. If you have a husband or a wife and children, you should, as a family, talk over your plans before starting.

How will your husband or wife feel about you caring for other people's children as well as your own? Will they enjoy the children and be a part of their activities when they are home? Do they have to work at night? If so will they be able to sleep during the day as the children play? Even if they aren't home during the day, they must be fully aware of what it will mean to both of you if you are to care for other children. Your whole schedule may change and it will be important for you and your husband or wife to know what this means and how it will affect your daily lives.

And what about your own children? How will they feel and act if they have to share your attention, their toys, and maybe even their bedrooms with other children? If they become jealous, will you be able to help them handle their feelings? If you have teenage children or college age children, how will they feel with younger children in the house again? Will having the children around disturb their studies, or make it difficult for them to invite friends home?

If there are other relatives in the home such as grandparents, how will this affect them? Will they be able to stand the commotion of children again? Will the change of routine in the home bother them too much? If they are home during the day, will they be able to relate easily to children in the home?

YOURSELF

"I'm not just a babysitter—I'm a day care mother. A sitter comes in for an hour and YOU tell her what you want for your child. I decide about meals, what time they are served, what to do, when and why . . . So I'm not a sitter—I'm a day care mother."[1]

Being a caregiver in a family day care home is a big job. You must think of your own feelings before taking on the large responsibility of taking care of other people's children. How do you really feel about a mother who gives up her children for part of the day? And can you really give to other children the care and attention they need without depriving your own chil-

---

[1] Sale, June S., "I'm Not Just a Babysitter," Pacific Oaks College, Pasadena, California, July 1971.

dren? Will you be willing to care for children of all ages? It's not unusual for a parent to seek care for children ranging from several months to eight or nine years of age. Such a mother would naturally desire to have all of her children cared for in the same home.

Before deciding to offer day care for children in your home you should ask yourself a number of other questions which will help you determine if family day care is really for you.

Ask Yourself

- Do I like and know enough about children? Can I stay with children for long hours and still be able to give each child the affection, security and protection he needs. Can I understand and respect the children well enough not to become over-involved with them or try to take the place of their mother or father?
- Do we have a warm family life that would give children the feeling they are welcome, secure and cared for?
- Am I in good health? Caring for children is hard work, physically and emotionally. Do I have the physical strength and stamina that will be needed?
- Can I handle accidents and emergencies calmly and efficiently?
- Can I be flexible enough to handle the surprises that come when children are around?
- Would I be able to give children the continuity of care they need? Young children, or children of any age tend to feel insecure and unloved if they are shifted around from home to home. They need the continual care of the same adults over a period of time. Can I continue to offer my service for a year, or until the children and their families no longer need it?
- What would I do for a substitute if I become ill, or have an emergency? Can I make arrangements with a substitute, one who can get to know the children and the parents before you need her, one who will carry out the routine nearly the same as you would?
- What kinds of satisfactions will being a family day care parent give me? Will it help me understand my own children better? Will it make me more secure to help

support my family? Do I really want the responsibility of someone else's child?

If after carefully considering these questions and talking them over with your family, you can decide that you would really enjoy and benefit from the experience of taking care of children in your home, then you can begin to plan to become a caregiver. You will need to think about many other things now—possibly re-arranging your house, licensing, budgeting, business and legal matters—all of the things involved in running a business.

LEGAL AND BUSINESS MATTERS

While family day care is not as complex as running a large business, there are some legal matters which you should be considering carefully. These involve insurance, taxes, budgeting and licensing. All, when taken care of properly, are for your direct benefit, and serve to protect you from unnecessary expense or liability.

Insurance

One of the first things you may have to think about is the insurance coverage on your home. Children are subject to a wide range of injuries, and while this type of insurance can be expensive it may serve to protect you and the children. Insurance coverage may be hard to find if you live in a building which houses another commercial business such as a restaurant, or even if you live in an apartment building. Almost all insurance companies will require an inspection of your home before they will consider coverage. If you have difficulty getting insurance, the agency which licenses family day care homes in your area (usually the Department of Social Services) may be able to help you. If you are working with an agency or Head Start program or other day care program, you may be able to get liability coverage through this group.

It is important to remember that coverage varies not only from company to company, but also from area to area. Shop around. Your own insurance company may give coverage in a nearby state or city, but not in your city or state. Some companies will cover an entire home, others require you to take out a separate policy for the day care children. Understand your policy clearly. *Do not assume* that an ordinary household liability policy will insure children in your care. Find out if your coverage is enough in the case of an accident involving more than one child. Furthermore, if you drive the children in your car, check to see if they are covered while in your car. You might also check with the parents to see if they carry any insurance on the child so that you can plan your own insurance needs. Be certain both you and the child's parents understand the insurance coverage, that both of you understand exactly when and where the children are covered—en route to and from the day care home, in the home or yard, or on neighborhood excursions.

Taxes

Some of the costs of taking care of children in your home may be deductible from your income tax. The following list suggests some of the possible deductions which you might be able to claim. These are *guidelines only,* and to be certain, you should check with a local Internal Revenue Service Office, legal aid society or tax attorney. In any case, you will have to maintain accurate records of payments for the items which you want to deduct. You should record all expenses immediately and keep receipts if you are planning to take the deductions.

possible deductible expenses [2]

1. Food and food preparation, equipment, utensils, etc.
2. Educational equipment (books, records, extra TV, etc.)
3. Special furniture (high chair, playpens, etc.)
4. Safety devices (socket covers, fire extinguishers, etc.)
5. Extra beds or cots and bedding
6. Expendable supplies (toilet paper, kleenex, laundry materials, disposable diapers, etc.)
7. Transportation (trips to doctor, etc.)
8. Utility expenses (extra heat, light, water used in the operation of the day care service)
9. Telephone (if an extra line is needed or if none existed before)
10. Insurance (if additional coverage is needed)
11. Advertising (cost of ads placed to recruit children)
12. Maintenance expenses and depreciation for any rooms used for day care.

Budgeting

Planning ahead for the expenses which you will have can save you money in the end. You will be able to check prices from various stores and to watch for special bargains. The following list gives you some of the items which you should include in your budget.

food. The number of meals and snacks you serve will depend on how long the children will be in your home.

supplies. Think about the cost of paper, crayons, paint, clay, scissors, paste and the other materials the children will use.

toys. Budget some money for the purchase and replacement of children's toys, blocks, dolls, books, puzzles, and other items such as a record player and records.

expendable items. Toilet paper, tissues, paper towels, disposable diapers are all costly items.

wear and tear on your house. Some wear and tear on your house is normal when young children are around. Think about the cost of repainting and other upkeep.

your time. You will want to consider the time you spend when figuring out your budget, and deciding on the amount of money you will charge.

transportation. Figure out the costs of car pools and transportation costs to your home if you pick up the children or take them on trips to local libraries, parks, doctors, etc., (if you and the children's parents feel you should assume these responsibilities).

---

[2] Two small pamphlets, "Your Federal Income Tax" and "Tax Guide for Small Business" may be useful. These may be obtained by writing to: Internal Revenue Service, Washington, D.C. 20226.

miscellaneous. Decorations, gifts, birthday presents, picnics for the families, family dinners, and holiday celebrations, are other items you might want to budget for.

training or schooling for yourself. Think about the cost of training courses, or schooling, that you may be able to participate in. Include the expense of transportation, books, pamphlets or magazines you will need.

To hold down the costs of toys and materials, always check to see what community resources are available. This list of community resources in Chapter IV will give you some suggestions. You may know of other resources in your own area which can also be helpful to you. Often it's worth your time to contact some of the local businesses such as hardware stores, stationery stores, drug stores, etc. to see if they have any free or inexpensive materials. You may not always be successful, but it is worth the try.

Once you have made out a budget, you will be able to figure out what sort of fee you should charge. In some cases you can charge a lower fee if you ask parents to provide such things as certain toys (bikes and other more expensive items), disposable diapers, and some of the books or puzzles.

Recordkeeping

As with any business there is a certain amount of recordkeeping. Keeping records will help you to evaluate yourself, your activities and the children's growth. They will be useful to you as you plan for the children's future in your home, and helpful as you plan interesting, challenging activities for the children.

If you are affiliated with an agency, it will usually provide you with forms to keep attendance records, and medical and conference information. In some areas, the licensing agency may ask you to keep some records in order to re-evaluate you and your program.

The records you will have to keep will vary from state to state and agency to agency. Whether you are affiliated with an agency or not, or are required to keep records for a license, you will want to keep some records for your own use. Some records you will want to keep are:

1. medical and health records on the children for your protection and theirs;
2. attendance records;
3. records of tax deductible items purchased —money spent for food, equipment and supplies;
4. insurance forms and records;
5. records for menu planning and food purchasing and preparing;
6. records of schedules of daily activities.

Sample records are found in the Appendix.

You may also wish to periodically assess the physical environment, your own performance and the developmental status of the children, and keep some records of this evaluation. You may find this a useful practice, one that will help you plan and build a quality family day care home. Such evaluations include the following:

The Physical Environment should be checked periodically, once every few months or so, to see if it is safe and efficient for the children and for you.

Check such things as:

● Is there a room which would be safer than one the children seem to prefer that could be made into more of a playroom?

● Are there any pieces of furniture that could be moved to make more room or to avoid accidents?

● Are there enough things for the children to climb on for physical exercise, either inside or outside the house?

● Are there enough toys and equipment so that children are kept interested and are not constantly fighting over the same toys?

Your Performance should also be checked periodically to see if there are ways you could improve your own activities.

Check such things as:

● Are you satisfied with the way the children respond to you, either when they are playing or when you have to give them directions?

● Are you able to plan activities for the children for each day or are you always trying to think about what they can do next?

- Are you able to get all of your own chores done or do you need to try another schedule to allow for more time for your own activities?

- Does your family seem to be happy with the arrangements?

- Are you happy with the arrangements or should you make some changes?

The Developmental Status of the Children should also be noted regularly and discussed with the parents. Some of the things you can look for and make a note on are:

- How is the child getting along with other children? Does he play with them, wait his turn, listen to other's ideas, suggest ideas to the others?

- How is he getting along with you? Does he seem happy? Is he eager to come to your home in the morning? Does he come to you when he needs comforting?

- What new activities is he engaging in? Is he eager to try new things? What things does he like to do best?

- Are his eating and sleeping habits changing?

- Is he more independent? Can he do things, such as dress himself, put his shoes on and zip his coat, by himself? Does he go outside by himself? Initiate activities on his own?

- Are there any special problems or things of interest that you should remember to tell his parents?

Meeting Licensing Standards and Agency Standards

Just as a center operating a group day care program is required to meet certain state, local or county regulations, so the family day care home is expected to meet certain established standards in certain areas of the country.

Usually the State or Local Social Services Agency is the group responsible for licensing family day care homes. A telephone call to the State Social Services Agency, listed under the name of your state in the telephone book, will most likely put you in touch with the proper licensing authority if one is available in your community.

Licensing protects you and the children you care for, and is really for your benefit and security. In some areas there are no regulations yet in effect for licensing family day care homes. In these instances you might obtain a copy of the Guides for Day Care Licensing from the Office of Child Development, Department of Health, Education, and Welfare, P. O. Box 1182, Washington, D.C. 20013. These requirements offer guidelines for the healthy care of children in homes, and might be useful in helping you to plan for quality child care.

Licensing regulations vary from locality to locality, however they are generally concerned with:

number of children

You really cannot take care of a large number of children and do a good job of giving each of them the attention and love they need. Be sure you count your own children when planning for a family day care home. The licensing agency usually limits the number of children that you can care for in your home.

your family

Often, to receive a license you and your family members must qualify in several respects. You, and all the members of your family, should be healthy, of good character and respected in your community. Some agencies may ask for references. In addition, you must demonstrate an interest and ability to care for children. Your doctor will certify that you and your family are free from communicable or infectious diseases.

your home

Your home may be a trailer, an apartment, a duplex or in a housing project. You can take good care of children anywhere, but often to qualify for a license there are certain conditions that must be met. The licensing agency usually looks to see if your rooms are well lighted, ventilated and heated. Paint needs to be free of lead; chipping or peeling paint might require repainting. Windows are usually required to be screened. Some times a licensing agency will help the family to meet the requirements. These might include getting a lock for a door, a guard in front of a heater, or rearrangement of existing space.

There are usually no specific requirements for the number of square feet of space needed for the children. Most standards however, suggest that there be some space for the children to play, eat and sleep comfortably. You will also need a sanitary water supply. If you have a well or spring, this would have to be checked by the sanitation department.

If you feed children in your home, there may be additional standards concerning the temperature of refrigeration for dairy products, the procedures for dishwashing and food preparation and storage.

activities in the home

Often the licensing agency will want to know what activities you have planned for the children. The daily activities in your home are of an informal nature, but the licensing agency may wish to see a definite schedule for the children which includes a balance between active and quiet play, a time for eating and resting, and some time to play outdoors.

the children you care for

The children you care for are often required to have a phyical examination before your home is licensed. This examination will show that the children are free from contagious or communicable disease and that they have received the required immunizations. It also gives you information on any special care the child will need.

THE DECISION TO OPERATE INDEPENDENTLY OR TO BECOME AFFILIATED WITH AN AGENCY OR GROUP

In many areas of the country today, family day care parents may have an opportunity to become involved with groups of other day care parents either through a local or state agency, or a private organization or group. Before offering day care in your home you should carefully consider whether you want to become affiliated with an agency or group, if there is one, or whether you prefer to remain independent.

There are a number of places where you can check to find out what types of groups may be in your area. In many states there is an agency, usually the local Department of Social Services, which grants licenses to operate family day care homes. These agencies may be very helpful in checking the possibilities of becoming affiliated with a group in your area. If they are unable to assist you, some other organizations which you might check are:
- Community Coordinated Child Care Councils (4-C)
- Day Care Federations
- United Way of America
- Local or State Social Service Agencies
- Religious Service Groups
- Federal Day Care Programs
- Head Start Programs
- Local Schools

While agencies and groups differ greatly, there are usually three types which may offer possibilities for affiliation. (See Chart on page 27)

Limited Affiliation With Public Agency

In many states there are public agencies such as the Welfare Department or Department of Social Services which may license family day care homes, as well as place children in family day care homes.

license affiliation

If you apply for a license but are not planning to care for children whose parents receive welfare, your relationship to the licensing agency will probably involve only the following:
- initial inspection by agency for license
- yearly re-inspection by agency for license
- referral of families looking for day care to your home

welfare agency affiliation

If you accept welfare children into your home, most likely the agency will perform the following types of activities:
- select children for you

- pay you directly for each child
- ask you to keep some records on children (attendance and others)
- may provide some training in child care for you
- may arrange meetings with other family day care mothers
- may provide materials, pamphlets or newsletters with information on child care

family day care system affiliation are a

In some areas of the country there is a growing number of agencies, both public and private, which is now operating "family day care systems." These agencies contract with a number of family day care homes to provide day care services for families. There are basically two types of systems, the "exclusive arrangement," and the "non-exclusive arrangement."

In a system which has an *exclusive arrangement,* your relationship with the agency will probably involve all or at least some of the following activities; the agency:

- trains family day care operator and gives "agency approval" to the home (similar to a license).
- selects children for the home and pays operator directly, either by fee per child or by set salary based on number of children.
- provides administrative services such as insurance, recordkeeping, evaluation and some purchase of equipment.
- provides homes with consultation and guidance and training.
- supervises homes and activities.
- provides or refers children to health and social services.

Under an *exclusive* arrangement, the family day care home accepts *only* agency selected children. There may also be other activities that the home must participate in under both arrangements.

If you belong to a system which has a *non-exclusive arrangement,* your relationship will probably involve all or some of the following activities as well as others not listed; the agency:
- recruits family day care homes.
- offers some training and supervision.

- pays for children directly either by fee per child or salary based on number of children in care.
- may provide health and social services or referral to services.
- provides consultation and assistance to homes.

Under a *non-exclusive* arrangement, the family day care home may accept children other than those selected by the agency.

Independent Operator Groups

There are many family day care operators who prefer to remain independent of any agency or family day care system, but who get together with other family day care operators to share experiences or to organize for mutual benefit. These independent groups are sometimes incorporated so that they can gain the benefits of group-purchase of items such as equipment or insurance.

If there are no such groups in your area, you may be able to get one started yourself by checking with the local licensing agency, welfare or social services department for names of other family day care operators near you. These groups may involve some of the following:
- referrals of children
- lower rates for group insurance or liability insurance
- meetings to share experiences and problems
- group trips or group purchase of equipment at lower prices
- some training in child care

While some family day care sponsoring agencies can offer a number of valuable services, they may also require you to take on specific responsibilities to carry out the goals of their program.

Deciding to Affiliate or Remain Independent

The decision to become part of a family day care system or affiliate with an agency or to remain independent (licensed or not) is a very important one. While there are many individual factors to consider, the overriding consideration must always be what would be best for the children and parents whom you will be serving.

benefits of affiliation

Among the benefits which can be derived from affiliation with an agency or system are:

- consultation and training by professionals in the field of child care
- provision of books, toys, equipment, whether for permanent use or loan
- assistance in recruiting children
- financial assistance including guaranteed fee from the agency for each child placed by them, and in some cases, financial help for home improvements, or additional food
- provision for substitute staff to care for children in case of your illness or an emergency, or even when you attend training classes
- assistance in identifying and using community resources
- assistance with financial or other problems you or children's parents may have
- regular contact with other family day care mothers
- help from volunteers or aides who may be able to come to your home to help with the children
- group trips sponsored by the agency
- transportation provided for the children
- lower cost or free group insurance or liability coverage

responsibilities

In addition to the benefits listed above, there are usually certain responsibilities which you will have to assume as part of an agency or system. For example, you will need to:

- keep up-to-date records on each child
- agree to abide by the rules and regulations of the agency—such as providing for a comprehensive educational program, health services and parental involvement in your activities
- take part in inservice training and other agency-sponsored activities
- agree to supervision of your activities
- charge fees set by the agency
- be willing to accept agency selected children
- arrange your own vacations and time off with the agency rather than on your own.

These benefits and responsibilities are, however, only general, and each agency or system sponsoring family day care programs will have its own way of operating which may or may not include them all. Discuss all of these aspects with the agency carefully before you make your decision.

Chart I
ORGANIZATION OF ALTERNATIVE DAY CARE AFFILIATION

The following chart indicates how some family day care homes may be related to various agencies.

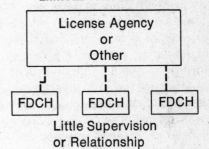

LIMITED AFFILIATION

License Agency or Other

FDCH   FDCH   FDCH

Little Supervision or Relationship

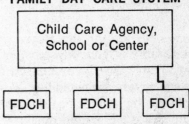

FAMILY DAY CARE SYSTEM

Child Care Agency, School or Center

FDCH   FDCH   FDCH

Close Supervision and Relationship

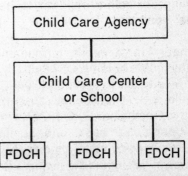

Child Care Agency

Child Care Center or School

FDCH   FDCH   FDCH

Close Supervision and Cooperative Programs

FDCH = Family Day Care Home

27

Summary

Before you make the final decision to begin offering family day care in your home you should be sure that you are satisfied that:

- Your family is completely willing to have other children in the home during the day, that your own children will not become jealous
- You can care for other children and not deprive your own children of the care and attention they need.
- You are flexible enough to handle the needs of several children at the same time, including emergencies and accidents without becoming upset
- You have the money to purchase the things you will need such as toys and materials
- You will be able to get, and afford, proper insurance on your home and the children
- Your house is safe for a group of young children, there is no chipping paint or lead base paint, drugs and poisons are out of reach, and electrical wires are covered and away from children
- You have considered whether you want to be independent or affiliated with a group or system of day care homes

The Office of Child Development is now conducting a Family Day Care Home Demonstration Program in six communities located in various parts of the nation. The purpose of the demonstration is to show that quality care can be provided in family day care settings when the caregivers are organized into a "system" of caregivers under the aegis of a central agency which can provide training, materials, equipment and management assistance support to the caregivers.

Preliminary information seems to indicate that family day care systems would provide quality child care at reasonable cost levels. The study, to be completed in 1974, will furnish data on operational costs and administrative mechanisms. The findings will be useful to those individuals and agencies throughout the nation responsible for the development and implementation of systems of family day care homes. Information resulting from the study will serve as a supplementary publication to this manual.

PREPARING YOUR HOME

Making it Safe

Wherever you live and whatever your home or apartment is like, you may want to make some changes in it before beginning a family day care program. Being a family day care parent means more than just loving children. It means that you give children the safety and protection they cannot provide for themselves. Part of the job of the family day care parent is to keep children safe so they can explore their world and trust it.

Take a walk through your home to see that your home is safe for children. Here are some things to look for and to remove before you begin caring for children:

- old wiring, extension cords that are overloaded or frayed or located where children could reach them;
- loose rugs, or rugs with frayed edges that could cause the children to catch a toe and trip, or slip as they play;
- ashtrays that children could reach as well as matches;
- plastic bags in which children can suffocate within a matter of minutes;
- windows should be locked and screened;
- stairways should be protected.

in the bedroom

A baby will spend a great deal of time sleeping, so the place in your home where the baby sleeps must be safe. Babies do learn to reach and climb and to grab things very quickly. Check to see that:

- all walls and surfaces are non-toxic—lead in paint can cause serious poisoning;
- heavy appliances like vaporizers and electric heaters are out of reach;
- radiators and heaters are protected or covered;
- there are no drafts from windows;
- venetian blinds or curtains with dangling strings are not near the crib—babies have been known to strangle themselves in these;
- diaper pins are out of reach of the baby;
- there are no toys and things you could trip on while carrying the baby.

in the bathroom

With all its attractions of running water and a toilet to flush, the bathroom is often an interesting place for young children. Be sure that it is really safe for the children in your home. Check to see that:

- drugs, medicines, razor blades, aspirin, mouth wash, soaps and sharp objects like manicure scissors are safely locked inside the medicine chest. If there is no place for a lock on the medicine chest, store them where the children cannot reach them.
- your bathroom door cannot be locked from the inside. Children often accidentally lock themselves in a room, and then panic. Remove the lock, put a hook lock high on the outside of the bathroom door, keeping it locked when the baby or toddler is in an exploring mood.
- any rugs are rubber-backed or non-slip.
- electrical appliances are removed from the bathroom—such as radios or electric heaters.
- bottles on the sink top or toilet tank top are removed. They can tip and break easily, or might tempt a child to taste them.
- there are plastic or paper disposable drinking cups, instead of glasses.

in the kitchen

You may often be in the kitchen fixing meals or doing household chores, and the children, wanting to be near you, follow you. Here are some things you might look for in your kitchen.

- keep pot handles turned to the back of the stove
- keep electrical wires from toaster and other appliances out of reach. Learn to remove the plug from the wall, rather than the cord from the appliance, coffee pot or whatever. A cord, still plugged into the wall, and dangling, not attached to an appliance, carries active electricity.
- keep a workable fire extinguisher in your kitchen; or have an extra box of salt and baking soda handy to smother fires
- if you have a gas stove be certain that the children cannot easily turn the knobs
- watch for long table cloths that the crawling baby might use to pull himself up on meanwhile pulling everything down on himself
- be sure all poisons, cleaners, furniture polish, etc., are stored high up out of reach of the children, and in a place separate from the food. If these things are stored within reach of the children, be sure they are locked up.

ARRANGING YOUR HOME FOR PLAY

"Oh, they play all over the house, but I did put some things away, and clear some space for them in the dining room." Most family day care homes allow children the same freedom to use all of the house as they allow their own family.

However, if there are several children in your home, they need some special space to play together, to make a mess in, and to call their own. If you care for school age children, they too may appreciate some corner reserved for them for their study or play. While you would not expect children, even your own, to stay in one place for the whole day or whenever they are playing, it is nice for them to have a place of their own to play in. You can find some space in your home for children's play by rearranging some things. A living room, with furniture moved to one end when the children are playing, gives them some floor space. A dining room table can be covered with some protective material and used for children's play.

Part of the kitchen can be cleared for children, allowing them to store their toys in one of the kitchen cupboards, or a well-lighted hallway could be used for play. Whatever space you select for the children's use, you should be sure that it is well lighted and heated, and safe for the children. There should be some covering on the floor, such as tile, linoleum or even carpeting, that can be cleaned. It may be helpful for you if the walls are washable and cleanable.

You will also want to make sure your house is arranged so that it allows the children the freedom they need. Leaving a bright, expensive glass figurine on the coffee table in the living room where the children play will cause you to constantly nag 'Don't touch,' 'Be careful,' 'Don't be so rough.' Removing it is far simpler. Simple things, like having a footstool by the sink so the children can get their own drinks of water, or a shelf of toys so the children can choose from what is available, will save you endless trouble, while creating a measure of independence in the children.

Think about other physical arrangements in your home. If you have a long hallway the children keep running through, or the children have found that they can run through the kitchen, living room and bedroom, making a complete circle, you might want to build a barrier, by moving a sofa, or other piece of furniture to make this space less attractive and inviting for the children to run through. This all depends upon your home and what you decide the children should and should not do.

GOOD ARRANGEMENT
...more play area
...no sharp table edges
...sofa safe from playing

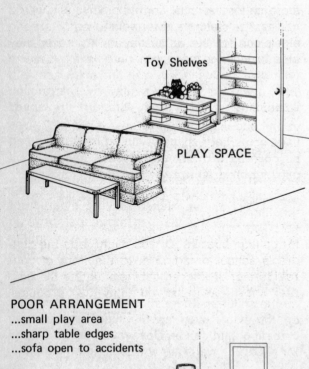

Toy Shelves

PLAY SPACE

POOR ARRANGEMENT
...small play area
...sharp table edges
...sofa open to accidents

Here are some suggestions for using space which may make it more useful for play. These ideas may also help you to think of other things you might want to do in your home, that will enhance the children's play, and fit your home.

Shelves

Shelves are handy when there are children playing in your house. The shelves let the children see all of the playthings and make choices for themselves, helping them to be independent. When a child has some shelves he is able to put his toys away as he finishes playing, and help keep some order.

Even small shelves can be useful, and can be cheaply and easily constructed in several ways. Wooden crates or cardboard boxes although becoming harder to find, may still be available at some markets. These, with edges sanded and a bright coat of paint and stacked one on top of another, make excellent play shelves. Plain wood planks can be placed on cement blocks to make handy low shelves.

Storage

With several children in your home you will need some way to store toys, preferably in a way that the children can do themselves. Rather than using just one box to pile everything in, many mothers have found other things to be more practical.

Gallon ice cream cartons, obtainable from a neighborhood ice cream shop, can be just right for storing a variety of toys and equipment. Each box can be used for playthings of a similar nature. Sorting all of the wooden beads, doll clothes and toy animals into separate containers will make it easier for the children to select the things they want to play with.

These storage cartons may also give the children the motivation to clean up, helping them to order and classify their world by putting all of the things that belong together into one container. If the containers are similar in size and shape, they can be easily stored and stacked away when the children are finished playing. Try wrapping them with paper that has adhesive on the back, or paint them in different colors.

Boxes for shoes, kleenex, cigars and other things can be used in the same way. Beer boxes are very handy, with flip top lids and strong sides, for storing children's toys. These can be easily stacked out of the way also.

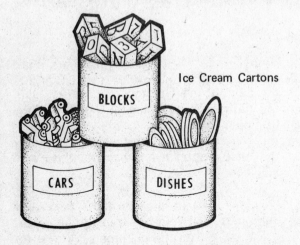

Ice Cream Cartons

FOR STORAGE

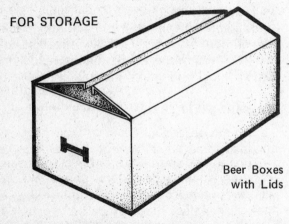

Beer Boxes
with Lids

Other containers for storing children's toys might be found at the thrift shop. An old chest of drawers, storage trays from stores, and other discarded furniture often provide handy places for children's toys and equipment.

Tables and Chairs

Young children spend a great deal of time on the floor, but there comes a time when they want to sit on a chair and work at a table. Somehow sitting at a table encourages children in a more serious type of play, such as putting a puzzle together, playing a matching game or painting a picture.

Children can easily use your kitchen or dining room table, or even a well-protected living room coffee table for these activities. A large phone book or sturdy cushion placed on a chair makes an adult-size table more manageable for the small child. You might want to find a child-size table and chairs for the children. A secondhand table, with legs cut down to size offers another possibility for a child-size table if you have room for it in your apartment or home.

Child-size chairs can be purchased or made. Small nail kegs from a local hardware store can be sanded and painted, and given a pad for the closed end forming a seat. Old footstools can be used as chairs, and of course, any type of wooden crate can be converted into a child's chair.

Wall Space

Don't forget how useful wall space is. You may be able to find a place in your home to hang a chalkboard for the children to use. A piece of cork or beaver board, attached to a wall, gives the children some place to display their drawings. The local hardware store may give you odd size sheets of wall board (ideal for bulletin boards). Or you might tape the children's school or art work to the front of your refrigerator or kitchen cabinets, letting the children know how much you enjoy their products.

...a nail keg chair..
...a plank nailed to chairs becomes a table.

chapter 2

What to Expect in Beginning a Family Day Care Home

FINDING THE CHILDREN

You've made the decision to offer family day care in your home; you've taken care of all of the necessary details and now you're ready for the children.

You may find the children by:

- contacting an agency that has a family day care system. Often these agencies may be able to refer families to you.
- placing an ad in the newspaper telling of your services. It's good to know that many newspapers will not accept such advertisements without first checking to see if you have a license.
- contacting local day care centers, Head Start programs, college campuses or factories and other places employing adults with young children. Existing schools and centers have a fair idea of the need for day care in the community based on their own experience, and may be able to refer.
- asking assistance from the local department of social services, agency for child development or other community agency serving children and their families.

YOUR FIRST MEETING

You, as the caregiver, together with the child's parents, must be certain you understand each other fully. It will be helpful for all, and may even save you embarrassment later, if you reach agreement on many things before you begin caring for the children.

Often your first contact with the family you will serve is by telephone. You can use this opportunity to share information about your program and to obtain some idea whether or not you could provide for the children. During your first telephone conversation ask about:

- the ages of the children;
- the days and the hours of the week they will need care;
- the general health of the child;
- the child's special interests, hobbies and activities.

At this time, arrange for the parents and the children to visit your home for an interview. When you meet with the children's parents for the first time you will want to put them at ease. The first interview is a two-way street. You are interviewing the parent to find out about the child you may be caring for, and to get to know his family. You are, in turn, being interviewed by the parents, who want to know if you are the 'right' person to care for their children.

Reaching Agreement

You and the child's parents will need to reach agreements on several points. You may want to put these agreements in writing, and have a small 'fact sheet' prepared to give to the parents to take home with them. A sample is given on page 34. The information on the fact sheet can be changed from time to time, but it will be helpful to both you and the parents as you begin your relationship.

In addition to any other concerns which you or the parents have, you should discuss and agree on the following points:

Weekly Fee

How much, when will the fee be paid, and in what form? Will you charge the same fee when the child is absent? Will you charge for holidays and vacation days? Will you charge the same fee for each child if they have more than one?

Will the fee include breakfast? snacks?

lunch? dinner? formula? What other services will be provided—taking the child to the doctor? Picking him up from school?

Hours of Service

You must agree on the time that the parent will bring the child to your home, and also the time he will pick him up. How much an hour will you charge for any extra time the child will spend with you?

Will you offer your services for evenings, weekends, holidays or summer?

Clothing

What clothing will you want the child to wear and keep at your home? Should he have an extra set of clean clothes? What about additional clothing to accommodate weather changes? Or accidents? How about diapers? Will you wash them? Is there a diaper service? What linens—towels, face cloths, sheets and pillow cases—will you ask the parents to provide?

Who Will Pick Up the Child

Inform the mother now, during this first interview, that you will need to know the names of the people who will be authorized to take the child from your home. It is wise to meet these people. If she, or the person who is designated to pick up the child, is unable to meet you first, establish at the start what procedures will be followed. Will the mother telephone you ahead of time, describing the person who will pick the child up? Will she send you a note, and will she give the person a note? Establish with the mother that her child must know the person who will pick him up in special cases. You may also want to know any person who is *not* allowed to pick him up.

Activities

You will also want to briefly discuss your activities with the child's mother and father, and reach agreement with them that you will provide certain equipment, toys, and regularly scheduled times for in and outdoor play, for meals and rest. You may want to tell them of your plans to take the children to the neighborhood library story hour, or to take them for walks in the neighborhood.

Substitutes and Your Vacation

Now is the time to discuss who will substitute for you when you are ill or cannot care for the child. The parents need to know what your plans are, and if possible, be introduced to the substitute. You will also want to inform them of your vacation plans, so they can make arrangements.

Emergency Care Procedures

Be prepared for emergencies and accidents. Establish right at the beginning the procedures you will follow in case of an emergency. You might be able to use this form to assist you in obtaining the information you will need. Ask the parents to fill it out, giving you a copy and retaining one for themselves.

IN AN EMERGENCY

I. If the child is ill, but does not require emergency treatment, you will be contacted at:

Parents' Home Address
NAME _____
ADDRESS _____
PHONE NUMBER _____

Father's Work Address

ADDRESS _____
PHONE NUMBER _____

Mother's Work Address

ADDRESS _____
PHONE NUMBER _____

II. If the child requires emergency medical care, the following procedures will be followed:

1. The child's family doctor will be called at:
   NAME _____
   PHONE NUMBER _____
   ADDRESS _____

2. If the doctor is not available, the child will be taken to the nearest city hospital emergency clinic which is:

   HOSPITAL NAME _____
   PHONE NUMBER _____
   ADDRESS _____

3. You will be called immediately.

4. In order to have a child treated for emergency care without the parent present, you will need a *notarized* form from the parents giving permission for treatment. See Appendix B.

III. Relatives or friends who are available in an emergency are:

1. NAME _____
   RELATIONSHIP _____
   ADDRESS _____
   PHONE NUMBER _____

2. NAME _____
   RELATIONSHIP _____
   ADDRESS _____
   PHONE NUMBER _____

Show the parents that you have, posted next to your telephone, the following numbers. Tell them you will now also post their telephone numbers and those of the child's doctor and clinic.

NEAREST AMBULANCE SERVICE
NEAREST HOSPITAL EMERGENCY CLINIC
NEAREST FIRE DEPARTMENT
NEAREST POLICE STATION
NEAREST ADULT SUBSTITUTE IN EVENT OF YOUR INCAPACITY

Establish and make clear the types of treatment you can give to a child in your care. Some states will not allow you to give any medication whatsoever to the child, or to care for an ill child. Talk over some of the things you might do in case the child becomes ill or has an accident, such as washing cuts, putting ice on bumps, or having the child rest.

Leaving

There comes a time when the family no longer needs your service. This may come automatically as the child reaches a certain age, but other changes, such as shifts in the family's jobs or plans, may account for the child leaving you. Each of you should decide on a reasonable amount of time to tell one another, and the child, if your service will no longer be needed.

Think about how you will tell the children you take care of when a child has to leave you. Sometimes children may be frightened if a child just disappears. Have a goodbye party for the child who is leaving, perhaps send him a post card or two, or in some other way help the other children to understand when one of them must leave you.

Family Day Care Fact Sheet

The weekly fee is _____
The fee is payable on _____, and it includes the following services:
_____
_____
_____
You may bring your child to my home at _____ and pick him up, no later than _____
A fee of _____ per hour will be charged for any additional time.
You will need to furnish the following items of clothing:
_____   _____   _____   _____
The following people, and these people only, will be permitted to pick up the child in case his mother or father cannot:
NAME _____
ADDRESS _____
PHONE NUMBER _____
RELATION TO FAMILY _____
NAME _____
ADDRESS _____
PHONE NUMBER _____
RELATION TO FAMILY _____

Other Agreements

There are other things that you and the child's parents will need to reach agreement on in order to work together for the good of the child.

What will the children call you? Mom? Pop Pop? Mrs. _____? Whatever you decide, you and the child's parents should agree. Does the family want their child to call someone else Mommy? Many family day care mothers ask the children to call them Aunt _____. Some younger family day care parents tell the child to use first names, while older family day care parents like to be called Grandma or Grandpa.

You might want to discuss your feelings and methods of discipline with the parent at this interview. Some people have strong feelings about discipline. Some parents may request that you spank a child when he misbehaves, and you must arrive at a clear understanding of what role you will play in the area of discipline. You are not the parent, and cannot be expected to do exactly as the parent does, but you should, at this very first meeting, explain to the parent, very simply, exactly how you do handle problems that arise. This gives you an opportunity to share knowledge with the mother that may be helpful to her.

When the child is of school age, you will want to know which of his friends he will be allowed to play with after school, where they live, and their phone numbers. Ask the parents now how they would feel about the child joining the local Brownie troop, or the arts and crafts program at the YWCA.

Sometimes your ideas on raising children in your home will conflict with the parent's ways of doing things. When this happens, you will need to work together to reach an agreement that will allow the child to feel secure with you and with his parents. You and the child's parents will need to work hand-in-hand; you both depend on each other. You use what she knows and she uses what you know to give the best care to the child.

You Will Want to Know These Things About the Child

There are many things you will need to know about the child and his family in order to give him the type of enriching experience outside of their home that will insure his fullest development.

Find out as much as you can about the way his mother takes care of him. Get her to tell you how he spends his day, what things he likes to do. Determine his food preferences and what foods disagree with him. It is also good to know if the child has been in a preschool or other family day care home, or how he was cared for before coming to you. If the child has been moved around a lot, he will need your help in feeling safe in your home, or if this is his first experience away from home he may need more time to adjust to you and your home.

You will also need to have medical information on the child. In the Appendix are samples of forms you might use to obtain all of the information you will need to have before giving care to someone else's child.

THOSE FIRST DAYS

"I think I'll go home now," determinedly announces the four-year-old on his first day in your home, exactly one-half hour after his mother has left, while the new two-year-old stands sobbing at the window calling, "Mommy, Mommy." These are very natural and normal reactions. The first days the child comes to your home may be very hard indeed, both for you, your family and the child. You can, however, by making plans, help the child to feel more comfortable with you, and ease his fears and anxieties about being separated from his parents.

Mother's Attitudes

Often children will copy their mother's and father's attitudes. If the mother is upset about having to leave her child, and is fearful and nervous, no cheerful words, no smiles can hide her worries from the child. Even babies can sometimes sense these feelings and become upset. Help the mother feel better about leaving her child for part of the day by:

- assuring her you will work hard to take care of her child.
- letting her know that you do not intend to take her place—you might tell her how the other children have learned to love you in

a special way but not in the same way they love their parents.

- telling her something about your program that may help to ease her—assuring her that you won't make her child eat broccoli, if he hates it, or telling her about the stories you will read and the things you will do.
- helping her to talk to her child about going to another home—she can tell her child something about you, the routines to expect in your home. Have her explain to her child that she will return at a certain time.

Children's Fears

Children will also need to have their fears of being separated from their parents considered. Some children may already know you or your children if you live in their neighborhood, but others will need to visit in your home, with their parents, in order to become acquainted with you. Often children have fears that they are unable to express. You might go slow and easy when you first meet the child and try, by making him familiar with you and your home, to relieve him of some of these fears. Usually the unknown is the thing that causes fear, but when the unknown becomes familiar the fears begin to disappear.

Help the children by:
- taking them on a tour of your home with their parents, showing them where they will play, where the bathroom is, etc.
- telling them about the things they will be doing. There is no need to make your home sound exciting or marvelous, the children just need to know, matter of factly, about the activities and routines in your home.
- planning a gradual separation period. It may be that you can arrange for the mother to stay with the children in your home for a few hours, or you might be able to arrange for the children to stay for only a part of the day until they become accustomed to you and your home.

Your Attitude

Usually with a pre-visit by the child with his parents, a shortened schedule for the first week, and the mother staying with the child for a short period of time, there are no real problems of adjustment. You might also visit the children's home.

However, you will want to plan very carefully for the first days a child is in your home.

- rather than giving the child all of the toys and things you have in your home, have a few simple things available, and encourage the parents to let him bring his treasured objects and toys to your home.
- find out what he likes to eat best and fix that for lunch, or fix a special snack.
- follow the regular routines you normally do, but watch for signs of fatigue in the child and make your schedule flexible enough to meet the needs of the child.

Your Own Children

Your own children, or even the children you regularly care for, may have adjustment problems when a new child enters your home. They may act their worst . . . whining, sulking, having temper tantrums for no apparent reason. It may be that these first days you have been paying more attention to the new child, and the others are feeling left out. The other children do not want you to divide your attention, giving more to another child. Try to reassure them, with your words and your actions, that they remain very important to you.

You will, just as you have prepared the new child, want to prepare the other children. You can:
- help them to understand their feelings. Tell them, "it may feel funny to see Aletha playing with your doll" or you ask them "how do you think we can help José to get to know us?"
- have the children decide ahead of time what toys and possessions they may want to share now, and what things they want to put away. Some children will decide to put everything away, leaving nothing to play with. If this happens, you can suggest that certain things be left out.
- respect the children's right not to share some cherished possession—a toy, blanket or object that is special for them.
- give them some responsibility for helping—have them take the new child on a 'guided tour' of the house, yard or apartment—or give them some other task that lets them know that they are participating in the life of your home and that they are responsible, capable persons.

Delayed Reaction

Everything is going smoothly, and the first week is over; the second was a breeze, with all of the children playing together happily, but now what has happened? The new child cries when his mother leaves him, and stands at the window sobbing for an hour after she has left. Sometimes, with the younger children, the excitement of a new place, toys, and playmates keeps them from feeling anxious and rejected for the first few weeks. But after the thrill has gone, and the cold light of day hits them, they come to the realization that they are being left! He has given up his mother in exchange for his time with you! He may realize that he is no longer a baby, he has been asked to grow up, and assume grownup responsibilities and behaviors. Accept these feelings, assuring him that he is important to his parents, to you, and to the other children. Give him something to do, help him enter the play group. Perhaps you can give him a plate of cookies to pass, or have him help you mix a milk shake for the children. Your understanding of why he suddenly objects to his mother's leaving as well as the matter-of-fact help that you give him allows him to gain his self-control and confidence.

GUIDING BEHAVIOR

And then there are those awful days! The baby whines, your own child yells at you, "no, no, no, I won't." The two-year-old bites the three-year-old, the preschoolers have been fighting all day, and the school age children come home quarreling and angry. No matter how well you have planned your day, there will be times when the children need help in learning to live comfortably with one another. Just as we all have had to learn, the children will need to learn how to recognize where their rights end and other's begin. All of the things we do to help children learn to respect others, to learn to live with themselves, and to live comfortably with others, might be called self-discipline.

There are some things which you can do to help children learn the lesson of self control.

Plan a Balanced Day

Plan the day so the children have plenty of things to do and choose among. Don't have every toy out every day. Put some toys away in the closet, and when the children seem bored, or nearly ready to fight, bring out the bag of forgotten toys. If you have planned something special for each day, like a trip to the store, some outdoor play, a special story to read, or making some cookies, your children will not have the time or interest to fight or get into trouble.

When you balance the activities, planning some quiet and some active, and when you challenge the children with new ideas, they are less likely to have problems living together.

Children also get into trouble when they have to wait. Look at your daily plans to see if the children will have to wait for long periods of time. Have toys ready for them, out on a table or in the play space, when they first come. Call them to wash for lunch when lunch is on the table, rather than asking them to wash their hands and then to sit and wait for 15 minutes until you finish fixing lunch. Don't ask them to wait too long for a special event. A day's notice is usually enough lead time. Waiting endlessly for some event makes the actual event seem anticlimactic. If you've waited three weeks to go to the zoo, the actual trip may be very disappointing. Even 5 minutes seems like a long time to a child, and might be just enough notice to 'wait' at the window for his mother. Any longer seems like an eternity.

Let Them Know Ahead

Let the children know what is coming next. Your regular routine of the day, with snacks, lunch, nap, all following a dependable, predictable order, helps the children to know what is expected of them next. Before you change an activity, give the children some warning. Tell them in a few minutes it will be time to clean up, or to go walking. When you say, "finish up the puzzle and then we'll eat," the children will have an easy time of obeying you. A clock or cooking timer can be a handy aid in setting those "last 5-minute" warnings. The bell, not you, calls the children to the next task.

If the schedule changes, be sure to tell the children why it has changed. "You will have to rest this morning so you can go to the park this afternoon."

Know Your Children

Know your children well. You can help them control their behavior when you understand them. John may suddenly begin sucking his thumb and sitting by himself in the corner. Does he need extra attention and reassurance that he is still loved even though his mother is not there? Understand that Julie is a very active child and needs to be busy. Give her a pile of diapers to take upstairs. Realize that José gets overexcited when he watches too much TV, and be prepared to calm him with simple, quiet activities.

When a child does misbehave, ask yourself if he is cranky because he's overtired, has nothing to do, or is he coming down with a cold? Also understand the normal behavior of young children. Know that the two-year-old says "No, No," to you because he must learn to become independent, and because it's often easier for him to say no than yes. Accept the fact that every child is active, and give them room for this normal activity. Say, "let's hop to lunch," or "who can jump and land very quietly."

Set Clear Limits

Set clear limits that the children can accept and understand, and that you will be able to stick to. If you have too many rules, neither you nor the children will be able to remember all of them. You will want to have some rules about hurting one another, "I will not let you hit, hurt, push, or bite another child, and I will not let anyone hurt you." And some simple rules about property, "You may not mark on the wall, break furniture, or destroy the record player," are manageable by the children. You might also need a rule about other people's things and say "You may not break the blocks down, or mark on her painting," and "He's using it; you can have it when he's finished."

When you have to remind the children about the rules, do so in a positive way. Often you can watch the children and before they actually do knock someone else's building down or hit a child you can say, "Sue, remember, you may not hit." Sometimes you will not even have to talk to help the children remember a rule; a look, a touch on the shoulder, a nod, or a smile across the room lets them know that you're watching them, ready to help them remember the rules.

Getting Them to Obey

"If only they would do what I tell them." Maybe the children need to be told in a different way. When you do want children to obey you, or to follow your directions, you will be more likely to succeed if you use language they can understand. However, before you ask children to obey you, be certain that your command is really necessary. Little children, just like adults, do not like to be pushed around. If they begin to feel they have no choices, and no say in their lives, they may begin to balk at your control.

You can give children choices, so that in obeying you they still feel they have had a say. Ask them, "Do you want to paint over here, or work with the clay?" "Would you like to wash your hands in the bathroom or right here outside?" "What book shall we read before nap?"

And if they are misbehaving, or in some danger, rather than just asking them to stop it, give them some alternative with your command to "stop." If you want the child to stop throwing the ball against your house, you can say to the child, "throw the ball here, on the sidewalk," or rather than saying, "don't climb the swing with a toy in your hand," say, "put your toy here, before you climb." These commands give the child some direction, and a clear idea of what he can safely do.

Encourage Feelings

Stop the children from hurting one another or damaging property, but encourage them to express their feelings. Children who have plenty of opportunity to paint, pound on clay, play in sand or water, or ride bikes as fast as they can, usually do not have to push or hit in order to feel important. The angry, fearful, or destructive child can be helped when you give him words to express his feelings, "I know how angry you are," and materials to take their feelings out on, "pound just as hard as you can on this wood."

Let the children see your feelings. Tell them when you're feeling angry or sad, or frightened or tired. Explain to them that today you've just 'had it' and you would like them to play quietly, or let them see you express your anger by getting mad. Tell them afterwards that everyone has feelings and that sometimes it's good to let them out, but you cannot hurt someone else.

They Will Copy You

The word discipline comes from the word disciple, which means learner or follower. Remember this, and know that the children will be following you, copying your every action. If you hit a child because he's doing something you do not like, the children will copy your behavior, and hit other children, or you, when things go wrong. If you yell and scream at the children to get your way, they will feel that yelling and screaming are the only ways to get attention. When you show respect for the children, by listening to them, letting them cry when they're unhappy, by caring for them, they will, in turn, learn to respect the rights and feelings of others.

Punishment

What about punishment? Should you ever punish a child? Should you hit or shake a child, or can you shame, scold, or ridicule them if they do something wrong? A good rule to follow is to avoid doing anything that you wouldn't want done to *you*. You might hold a child's arm to prevent him from striking a child, or even pick up and bodily remove him from the group, holding him firmly until his anger has passed, or saying to him, "come and sit over here with me until you're ready to play without hitting." Removing the child from the group is helpful but remember not to lock him in a room by himself. When he is angry or upset he may hurt himself or your property. If you do remove a child for a few minutes, ask him to be with you until he decides he is ready to return to play. Try not to ask him to sit out for too long a time. A few minutes is all he may need to gain control of himself again.

Catch Them Being Good

So often we only pay attention to the children when they're doing something wrong. Notice the children when they're "good"; try saying, "you've been a big help today," "what a good job you've done getting ready for nap." Giving children attention when they're acting their best encourages good behavior, just as giving them attention when they've misbehaved may reinforce more misbehavior.

Here are some problems and some of the ways you might be able to deal with them.

Do You Have a Fighter?

If you do, he probably is fighting because he is afraid he is no good, afraid of the other children, or unsure of himself.

You can:

Separate him, saying, "come and sit with me, I cannot let you hurt anyone," or redirect his attention, "kick the tire," or distract him, "here is a red truck to play with."

Next, help him to talk about his angry feelings, "I know how you must feel . . . tell me." Always show that he is liked, never meet his hostility with yours, give him success with people and things so he doesn't have to fight for them.

Do You Have a Show Off?

If you do, he may be saying, "I'll show off to be noticed," "nobody loves me," "I'm not as good as other people."

You can:

Praise him for all of the good things he does. Make him feel important before he begins to show off . . . "didn't Carmen eat well today?" And you can ask him his opinion of things he really can decide, "Do you want chicken rice or noodle soup for lunch today?" helping him to feel respected.

Do You Have a Do-Nothing?

If you do, he may be saying, "I'm afraid I'll fail, so I won't do anything," "I'm afraid of others," or "I'm overwhelmed with everything, I don't know where to start."

You can:

Invite the child to do just a little thing with you, "take my hand and walk to the tree with me." You can give him a simple project that you know he can succeed with, "take this diaper to the bedroom," or you can sit with him quietly, talking to him, telling him he is good.

Do You Have a Storyteller?

If you do, he is probably saying to you, "I must defend myself with a story because I'll be hurt if I tell the truth," or, "I will lie to stay out of trouble, and hide my inability." Young children sometimes have difficulty knowing the difference between fact and fancy, so you might consider this.

You can:

Ignore some of the tall tales, if the child is very young and has no concept of fact and fancy, help him to tell the difference. Say, "this is a true story, it really happened," or "the story of Little Red Riding Hood is not true, it's pretend to have fun with."

You can give him opportunities to achieve without lying, and you can tell him, "you don't always have to make it different, I will understand how it really was."

Do You Have a Taker?

If you do, he may be saying to you, "I don't have what the other children have, so I take it," "I'm bored," "I don't get attention from you so I will steal something to get your attention."

You can:

Provide the things he really needs, and determine whether he does know that some things belong to other people. Try always to approve of him, but not his stealing. Try to give him your attention when he's being good, and help him to make friends with the other children and join in the activities.

Do You Have a Curser?

If you do, he may be trying out new words he's heard, annoying or testing you, or simply trying to act "big."

You can:

Be very casual, and not give him attention for saying these words. Often by ignoring such language, the child has no desire to repeat it. Help him to feel big about himself on other ways so he won't have to use this language in order to feel big.[3]

ILLNESS

What to do with the sick child? Mothers cannot take too many days off from work, but where should the sick child go? For many years the policy has been to isolate the sick child from other children, and you may still feel this is best. However, different methods of dealing with the ill child are being tried successfully.

Some physicians are suggesting that the ill child be allowed to stay in the family day care home, perhaps in a separate room, or away from the other child. Doctors have found that the child who is ill has already spread the disease before his symptoms actually appeared. So the other children have usually been exposed to the disease before anyone was aware of the fact that the child was ill.

You must, however, be very careful about giving children medicines. Some states and licensing agencies will not permit you to give any medication to any child in your care. Others, however, will allow you to give medication to a child at the physician's direction and the mother's request. If this is the case, be certain that you have a written statement from the parent describing the procedures to follow, and go over these directions with the parent so both of you clearly understand what you are to do. (See Appendix B.) It is best, however, not to give a child medication of any kind, including aspirin, cough drops, syrups, cold pills, without a doctor's prescription and at the request of the mother.

Children who are recuperating from an illness may need special consideration, and those who are feeling much better, but still must limit their activities, will require something special to do.

---

[3] Adapted from *Children's Behavior*, Child Welfare Division, Florida State Department of Public Welfare, 1958.

You might:

Keep a surprise bag ready for ill children. It doesn't matter what's in it, just so it's different, and suited to the age and developmental level of the child. One family saved all of the tiny things that came in cereal boxes to put in this bag, and another saved the junk mail that contained stickers, envelopes, and coupons.

A new book, a small package of new crayons and a small notebook, some colored construction paper or old greeting cards and a hole punch, a magnifying glass, a kaleidoscope or binoculars will keep the child quiet and interested.

Staple some sheets of paper together and call it the 'chickenpox' book or whatever, and give this to the child recovering from the chickenpox. Have him draw all of the things he thinks of that remind him of having the chickenpox.

Give the child a mirror, and let him make designs around the room, or a flash light that works in a darkened room to draw patterns with on the ceiling.

Finger puppets, dolls too small for regular play, and paper dolls might also be appropriate. Or give them a box of cut up straws and a long shoestring and let them make necklaces.

Some people feel that keeping the sick child with the other children helps everyone to accept illness, and to become more aware of healthful living. You, your agency, the parents of all of the children you care for, as well as the licensing agency, will be involved in the decision to care for, or not to care for, sick children.

ACCIDENTS

Are you ready? Do you have a routine for handling accidents? Plan ahead, and accidents and emergencies can be handled in a routine, effective manner. First, always plan with the parents for handling accidents. Next, plan with yourself and the children.

Ask yourself what you would do if there were a fire. Do you have a fire extinguisher, and do you know how to work it? What if a child

swallowed cleaning supplies? Do you have the number of your nearest poison control center? Think to yourself, what would you do if a child fell and broke a bone? Prepare yourself by attending free first aid classes at the local Red Cross. It is important to have a *written plan* for emergency where you or anyone else in the home can see it.

Without alarming the children, teach them to plan for getting out of your house or apartment in case of emergency. There is no need to frighten the children, but you can, without alarm, have a practice fire drill, saying "We don't think there will be a fire, but let's practice what we would do in case of a fire. Knowing what to do will keep us safe." Another day you might say, "Let's think about what we would do if someone were hurt. Knowing what to do if someone were hurt will help to keep us safe." Make sure that every new child practices for an emergency soon after they arrive.

When an accident occurs, you must first care for the child who has been injured, but you also have a responsibility to the other children. After the injured child has been cared for, and is comfortable, you might talk with the children, asking them why they think the accident happened. "Was there a block in the way of the bike?" "How high did she climb in the tree?" "What can we do next time to see that no one else falls from the bike?" It sometimes happens that other children feel they are to blame. Even if they are, they need to be reassured about the part they played in the event. It is rare that one child really intends to cause a serious injury to another, even if he was provoked or angry.

Occasionally an accident occurs where you need outside help. Have the following numbers posted by your phone: Police, Fire Department, Hospital, Ambulance, Physician, and a Responsible Relative or Friend who could help you in case of an emergency. It might be wise to keep an envelope with the amount of money it would take to pay a cab or an ambulance to take you to the hospital, sealed on a shelf near the phone.

Follow the procedures for handling the accident that you have agreed upon with the child's parents.

RELATIONSHIPS

Relating to Parents

You call them *MY* children and they call you "Momsie" or "Pop-Pop." You care for them, feed them, wash their scratched knees, wipe their noses, and enjoy watching them grow and develop. And yet they are not your children, and you are not their mother or father. You are in the unique position of being LIKE a mother or father to the children, but not in fact. You must always remember that the children you care for belong to someone else.

Put yourself in the position of a mother or father leaving your child with someone else for the entire day while you went to work. Would you feel jealous toward the person who gets to spend the whole day with your child? How would you feel if your child were to call the person you left him with "mommy"? What if your child cried when it came time to take him home?

You can see that it is important for you as the day care parent to respect the child's own family. The child must feel and know that you respect him and his entire family. Remember, you must communicate to the child that you know his mother and father are the most important people in his life.

Children will 'catch' your attitude of concern for their parents as you remind the child about his mother and father during the day. Refer to the children's parents during the day. "That bus in just like the one your mother rides to get to work." "Let's put that picture here, then your mother can take it home with her."

You might ask the child if he would like to put a photograph of his parents on the refrigerator door, or in a frame, to remind him that you care about his entire family. Perhaps the children are old enough to draw or paint a family portrait for your kitchen.

Ask the mother and father if they can receive phone calls during the day at work from their child. You would not have the child call them daily, but perhaps once a month or on some special occasion. The children could be taught to dial the phone themselves, and to ask to speak with their mother, perhaps using the parent's first and last names. This activity keeps the children 'in touch' with their mothers and fathers, and it also gives them valuable experiences in the proper way to use a telephone, and speaking clearly enough to make themselves understood by others.

Encourage the children to talk about their parents during the day; ask "What do you think mother will be eating for lunch? Let's remember to ask her when she comes." "Does your daddy like onions on his hamburgers too?"

Ask the child to think ahead and to happily anticipate his evenings and weekends in his own home. "Take this book home with you and read it to your mother before you go to sleep." "Your mother told me that in two more days she was going to take you to the zoo. What will you see there?"

Communicating With the Child

Many of the activities you do with the children during the day will communicate to them and the parents exactly how much you think of them.

- When the child enjoys a special dish, perhaps the way you make rice and sugar, you could write the recipe on a card and give it to the mother that evening with a sample of the dish.
- You could ask the mother for her recipe for the child's favorite dish, and make that for him.
- When the children paint or draw pictures you can write a note on them, telling the parent what the child told you about his picture, or how he made it.
- If you and the children enjoy a certain story, ask the child to take the book home with him and share the story with his mother and father.
- Whatever the occupation of the parents, see if you can find something for the children to play with that will help them to act out their parents' occupation. This may help the child understand what his parents are doing while he's with you, and may even encourage him to think to the day when he will enter the world of work.

going home time

Remember the child that cried when he

42

first came to your home? He may be the very same child that will cry and scream when it is time to go home with his parents. You can help to prevent this from happening by preparing the child for going home. You may want to establish certain routines, such as cleaning up, washing or changing clothes, or reading a favorite story before going home.

It helps to tell the children ahead of time, very matter-of-factly, that "now it's time to go home. Put your things away, and then we'll read together until your mother comes." Have the things the children made during the day ready on the table or nearby to give to the parent. Think about the things you want to tell them about the child's day, talk it over with the child . . . "think of the thing you had most fun with today so we can tell your mother when she comes." When the parents arrive, you may want them to do most of the talking and asking questions of the child so that they feel in command again.

Communicating With the Parents

You must also communicate your concern and respect to the child's parents. To guard against the parent's feelings that you are supplanting their role as mother and father, you can ask them for their advice and act on their desires. Ask the parents about the children. "Are there some special things you want me to do for Valerie?" Before you plan any really different activity, communicate with the parents. You may be thinking about taking the children to the circus, zoo, or art museum, only to find out that the parent is planning to take a day off from work to take his children there. Or you may want to give the child a certain special toy—a plastic horse or something he has been wanting for a very long time. Before you do, check with the child's parents to be certain that they have not already purchased the item and are saving it for his birthday or some other time.

Parents are your best resources, and have valuable suggestions for you. Ask them to suggest places to take the children. Perhaps they know the baker, and can help you to arrange a trip to see what happens in the back room of the bakery shop.

Try to use every opportunity to communi-

cate with the parents. Parents' mornings and evenings are rushed times. In the morning the parents are trying not to be late for work, and in the evenings when they pick the children up they are in a hurry to get home to fix dinner, clean, and shop. Nevertheless, even these rushed moments, when the parents bring and pick up the children, can be used by you to establish communication with the family.

First plan your schedule so you are free of any other activity when they pick up the children. If you are not trying to fry bacon and eggs, or prepare dinner, you will be more likely to give your complete attention to the parents when they come. Talk with the mother when she comes in the morning, "How was your evening?" "How is his cold?" And again, in the evenings, be ready to give all of your attention, even if it's only for a moment or two, while the child is putting on his coat and gathering his things together, to talk to the mother and father. "How was your day?" "We had fun today, ask Irving to tell you about making bread." It's helpful, before the parents actually arrive, to think of at least one good thing to tell them about their child and the things he did that day. Telling the parent something positive each day about her child communicates to the parents that you respect and value them and their children, and it creates positive feelings between you.

Even though you do make full use of these daily contacts, you will also want to establish some time to communicate more fully with the child's parents.

- A short telephone call to the parents after the children are in bed helps you keep in touch and helps you to understand the child and his family better.
- You might be able to set aside an afternoon a week or once a month, for the parent to stay for a few extra minutes after work. Over coffee you can discuss the child's progress and your mutual concerns, as well as plans for the future.
- Plan a dinner or picnic lunch together. It may be possible for the mother to join you and the children for a special lunch once in a while.
- Invite the parents to spend some time with you and the child in your home. There are often occasions when parents will be able

to spend a few hours with their children in your home.

These occasional visits to the home when the child is present, further establish a link between the parent and the family day care home.

When you are communicating with parents, you might remember some of the following hints:

be positive

Parents often are accustomed to hearing negative things about their children from others. The neighbors usually do not run to the parents to tell them how lovely their children acted, but they are quick to tell them when the child stepped on their flowers. Focusing on the "bad" is discouraging and angers the parent. Focusing on the "good" helps people to feel comfortable, safe, and free to talk. Discuss the work the child has done, the progress he has made.

be ready to listen

Don't feel you have to do all of the talking during a formal conference, and don't feel you have to be so business-like that you can't be informal and friendly. Let the conversation wander, being prepared to bring it back to the child again.

Let the parents talk about themselves and their children. Hear what they have to say about you and your program. You will learn a lot. Ask the parent questions, let her share her concerns, her worries, and her opinions with you.

plan ahead

Some things can be very important to remember when you talk with parents. You will want to review and update the following:
- health and medical records
- accident and emergency procedures
- addresses, phone numbers of contact persons, and parents' work
- progress of the child
- eating, sleeping, and toileting habits
- discipline techniques and methods
- plans for the future
- when the child will be going to school
- should he stay in your home when he starts school?
- what activities and things will be prepared for the future?

be professional

Often you and the child's family can become very close. You will share so many things together, and have so many things in common that it will be natural for the parents to begin to confide in you, and to bring to you their personal problems. It's best if you retain some business-like attitude. It is often best for the children, you, and the parent if you try not to discuss or become involved with personal family problems.

Also be professional about the other children in your care. Focus on the parent's child. They do not want to hear about the other children you are caring for, and do not want you to tell the other parents everything about their child.

chapter 3

Developmental Needs of Children

As different as can be, and yet, every child in your home is alike in many ways. Every child grows and learns, every child goes through the same stages of development, and every child has the same basic needs that must be met.

All Children Need to Trust and Feel Safe in the World

Everyone needs to feel safe in his world, but especially children. Babies who are so helpless and even older children, who still depend on someone to take care of them need to feel secure and free from fear—they need to learn to trust their world. The caregiver helps children to feel secure and safe in their world by:

- treating each child as an individual—feeding each child when he's hungry, letting each rest when tired, and comforting each when tired or frightened.
- doing things in much the same way their own mother or father would do for them so the children will not be fearful or confused by a very different way of living.
- building daily routines that children can depend on, so they will know that lunch comes after play, rest after lunch and snacks at certain times of the day.
- letting each child know they and their families are loved and respected by telling them often, with words, or a hug, smile, pat on the back, how much you do appreciate them.

All Children Need to Express Feelings and to Feel Understood

Children's feelings are close to the surface—they scream when they're unhappy, hit when angry, and burst into giggles when something delights them. In the family day care home children are encouraged to express their feelings by:
- giving them the words needed to talk about their feelings . . . "you must have felt very angry at Jo," "didn't you feel good when you did that?"
- accepting their feelings, "I know how you feel," "you really were angry" and show them that even if their feelings get out of hand, you still respect them.
- showing them how they can express their feelings by playing, painting or drawing a picture, or just by running as fast as they can around the block.
- letting them know that everyone has feelings, letting them see you when you are angry, frustrated or happy, showing them that you accept your feelings and let them out without hurting or disturbing others around you.

All Children Need to Feel Independent

The same children who are so dependent on you must also feel that they are independent, that they can do things for themselves, and that you trust them to do so. Children in a family day care home learn to feel independent when they:
- can do things for themselves . . . dressing, washing, picking up after play.
- help the caregiver with real jobs—carrying diapers, baking a cake, or setting a table.
- have some place for their own personal things, and a place where they can be alone for a while if they want to.
- are allowed to play with others in the neighborhood, join a neighborhood group or go to the playground without you when they are old enough and their parents have given permission.

All Children Need to Feel Successful

Nothing succeeds like success! Everyone needs to feel successful and the more successful a child feels, the more he wants to try to do.

45

The caregiver helps children to feel successful by:

- giving them things they can do easily at first—puzzles they can put together with ease, games they can play by themselves—and then after they've succeeded, giving them more challenging things to do.
- having materials available for the children to build and construct with so they can have the satisfaction of creating something.
- helping the school children with their homework, finding books they can read without help.
- praising the children when they have accomplished something, no matter how small the accomplishment.

All Children Should Feel Good About Themselves

When children's basic needs of feeling safe, of expressing feelings, of becoming independent and feeling successful are being met in the family day care home, children begin to feel good about themselves. Children feel good about themselves as you:

- stop what you are doing to listen to them, or to admire their work.
- respect their ideas and wishes—making the food they like for lunch, letting them choose their activities and friends.
- let them know they can count on you to be available to help them work out their problems, or to set consistent, safe limits for them.
- point out their positive characteristics, complimenting them on the good things they do.

All Children Need to Learn to Get Along With Others

One of the most pressing needs a human being has is the need to learn to get along with others. Every child, and every person, needs to learn how to develop ways of getting along with many others.

The family day care home, with a few other children, and a few dependable, familiar adults, helps a child fulfill his need for social contact. In the family day care home, the children:

- learn to develop an awareness of the needs of others as the caregiver tells them, "don't

hit him, you'll hurt him," or "not so loud now, the baby is sleeping."
- have the opportunity to play with others, both younger and older than himself.
- learn to work through and handle conflicts —Susan wants to play with the car Robert brought from home, Karen won't let David play with her block building, and Aletha wants to use the record player while Robert is using it.

With the help of the caregiver who teaches the children the skills they need to work with, and share with one another, children learn to live with others.

All Children Have Physical Needs

Usually a healthy child is a happy child—a child who is able to learn new things and who can get along with others. The family day care home meets the child's basic need to be healthy by giving him the protection he needs and a safe environment to live in. In a family day care home the child's physical needs are met by:

- well-balanced, nutritious meals and snacks.
- a daily plan that allows children active and quiet activities, with time for exercise and rest.
- attention to the child's medical needs—keeping the child's medical records up to date, or even helping the parents locate medical care suited to their needs.
- caring for the ill child.
- establishing habits of healthful living—washing hands before eating, keeping the home clean, safe and orderly.

All Children Need to Learn About the World Around Them

The need to know about the world is crucial. The more children and adults know, the more secure they feel and the more successful they are. The family day care home helps children to learn, and gives them knowledge of their world. In the home the children are able to:

- explore and discover the world for themselves in a safe, comfortable environment.
- be allowed to play with the pots and pans in the kitchen cupboard because all dangerous things are removed, and the school age child is allowed to, with his parent's permission, join clubs, or explore

the neighborhood, learning even more about the world.

- have their questions answered in simple ways, gaining information about everyday things.
- enjoy many experiences, to listen and talk to others, to hear stories or to read books, and to use language.
- learn to solve problems, to find out about things, to experiment and explore the world around them through play.

PLANNING TO MEET THE NEEDS OF CHILDREN IN A FAMILY DAY CARE HOME

Each of the children's needs must be met in your home. When planning daily activities, ask yourself if all of the children's very basic needs will be fulfilled. No one need can be neglected for they are all linked together. A child who has never felt safe, has never learned to trust his world, can never learn to be independent. A child who doesn't know how things work in his world, or doesn't have the language to express himself, is not able to feel good about himself, for he won't be able to do things.

If a child doesn't learn to develop social skills, and learn the give and take of living with others, he cannot find out more about his world or learn new things, for his fear of people will hinder him. A child who is hungry or malnourished, or in poor health is not able to learn —he can only survive. Plan carefully to meet each child's social, emotional, physical, and intellectual needs.

Probably you will have to plan different things for different children, for although children have the same needs, they are also very different, and sometimes their needs must be met in very different ways. True, all children grow and develop and all children learn, but each child grows and develops at his own speed— each follows his own timetable, each will be learning different things in his own way.

You can learn to recognize these differences in your children, and know each of them so well that you understand exactly what type of activity is suitable for them and how to help each one develop into a successful person.

A caregiver who loves her children takes

the time to carefully plan for them, organizing their days so they have a rhythm and pattern of meaning giving the children all of the experiences they need to grow. Some things the caregiver would want to include in the day are:

- a balance of activity and rest—such as playing outdoors and reading
- a balance of individual and group activities —such as working a puzzle by yourself or playing house together as a group
- a balance of quiet and noisy activities— such as watching TV and playing hide and seek
- established routines for toileting, resting and eating which encourage health habits and give children the security of a well ordered, and preplanned sequence of events—such as washing before lunch, eating and resting after lunch
- large blocks of time which allow children to make choices and to explore their environment—letting the children play outdoors for a long period before making them come inside
- for the school age child, a balance of free time, active play and educational activities and a place to invite his friends
- flexibility to take advantage of special activities or occurrences and to keep children from feeling pressure—going to the park on a sunny day, letting a child play with the blocks all day if he wants to

The activities a caregiver plans for the children change as the children grow and develop. The ages of the children, the time they spend in the home, the type of toys and play equipment available, and the individual backgrounds of the children are all considered before the mother plans her daily activities.

Routines in a Family Day Care Home

When you know what's coming next, you are more comfortable, relaxed and sure of yourself. It's important that the children also know what's going to happen next in the family day care home, and be able to depend on a certain order in their day. The simple routines of eating, sleeping and washing can serve as a framework around which the child's day is organized.

Even the very youngest toddler soon

47

comes to realize that when he comes to your home he'll have something to eat and then he'll play, and that before lunch he will wash his hands, and after lunch he'll nap. These activities will become familiar aspects of his day, things he can anticipate and understand.

He can tell time by their happening. Not that it will make any difference to him if lunch is served at 11:00 a.m. or noon, but he will know that nap will come afterwards, giving him a sense of order and a feeling that he can depend on his world. When children know what's going to happen next, and can depend on it happening, they begin to feel in control of themselves, and their world. Children need to depend upon the familiar before they can reach out to the new.

These routines, washing, eating, sleeping, may also serve as valuable learning experiences. They help the child to learn habits of health and safety, as well as to develop healthy attitudes about his body and its functions.

Habits of cleanliness and personal hygiene are practiced routinely throughout the day. Many of these are taught by your example. Children watching you brushing your teeth, using a handkerchief, washing your hands after changing the baby's diaper, washing a cut or scratch, will naturally want to copy your behaviors.

resting

Children living together in a group, active and playing together for most of the day, must balance their activity with rest.

Children appreciate and enjoy resting, and cooperate fully in taking naps when:
- they are not punished by being "sent to bed." If bed is used only for resting, children who have been playing and working hard, think of it as an inviting, comfortable and welcome place.
- the caregiver helps the children to understand the importance of resting and napping by saying to them, "resting helps us to grow," "your body needs to rest to stay well" or by explaining to the cranky child, "I think you're tired, that's why you're not getting along, let's see if a rest will make you feel better."
- everyone in the home rests. The caregiver

and the older children may not want to actually sleep during naptime, but it also can be a time for some quiet activity for them.

Usually children will rest several times during the morning and the afternoon. You might serve juice and apple slices while you read them a story. Some toddlers may be giving up morning naps, but they'll still require a quiet time alone. And others, even preschoolers and school age children, may need to have a place to "get away from it all," to stretch out, to think by themselves, each morning or afternoon.

Most young children, in addition to these "quiet" activities, will require a full, stretch-out nap following lunch.

Regular beds, folding cots that can be stored under adult beds, or floor mats might be used. Not all of the children will sleep, or require the same amount of resting time. Every child should be allowed to select the type of rest he desires, as long as it doesn't interfere with the rest of others, and as long as it gives him relaxation. When children are allowed to select their own type of rest, the battle between the adult who knows what's good for the child, and the child who knows "you can't make me sleep," is eliminated.

Usually the lunch hour signals rest, and is quiet enough to serve as a preparation for nap. You might want to establish some routine following lunch such as reading a story, listening to a record, or looking at pictures.

Let the children sleep as long as they need to. Children who have had sufficient sleep during the day are more likely to be able to fall asleep in the evening. On waking, a snack, or something refreshing to drink might be waiting for them in the kitchen.

Children coming to the home following a busy day at school will need some time to be quiet and restful. They may want to read, listen to records, or just be by themselves for a few minutes.

toileting

Each child, as every adult, has a different

pattern for elimination. Usually in a family day care home, with the younger children observing the older children using the bathroom, few toileting problems arise.

With infants and children under the age of two, the best procedure is to change their diapers frequently, not allowing any child to stay in soiled diapers. Keep a separate pail for each baby you care for, unless you use disposable diapers. When you are caring for children in diapers, be very certain to wash your hands after changing each baby, and carefully dispose of the soiled diaper, flushing it out, and placing it in a pail of soapy water.

Most children under two years of age will not have learned to control their elimination. Around the age of 2, you and the parents can decide when to teach the child to use the toilet.

In toilet training it's helpful if that both you and the parents agree on the procedures to be followed. If you do things very much differently from the child's parents, it will be confusing to the child, and he might not know what is expected of him concerning toileting. Ask the parents what words they use in their home to describe elimination, and use the same words with the children.

During and after the training period, you can assume some responsibility to remind the children to go to the bathroom. A young child, absorbed in his play, may forget about going to the bathroom. When you see a child holding himself, jiggling around, or you know that he hasn't gone to the bathroom for sometime, you can say ". . . come in now and go to the bathroom" and take his hand, and lead him to the toilet.

Accidents do happen, and when they do, matter-of-factly clean up the child, help him into a quick change of clothing, and see that he gets back to play, or help him to re-enter the game.

School age children will need to have their privacy guaranteed when using the bathroom. The preteen is now both ashamed and proud of his body changes and his mixed feelings may lead to his becoming extremely modest. This privacy needs to be respected in the family day care home.

staying healthy

Staying healthy is hard work for the young child who must learn how to dress for different types of weather, how and when to wash, and how to keep play spaces orderly in order to avoid accidents.

washing Most young children are eager for washing up activities. They love to play in the soapy water and may wash themselves, the mirror and the wall. Encourage the children to do their own washing up, checking to see that your water supply never becomes dangerously hot. You may need to help the two's learn to wash their hands. Just saying, "time to wash," may leave them wondering what to do next while standing at the sink.

Washing is a good time for children to learn the names of their body parts. You can say to the children while they wash, "here's some dirt on your *wrist, thumb, elbow,*" or "how clean you've washed your *cheeks, ears* or *forehead.*"

Try to establish the idea that it is important to wash hands before eating and allow the children to take as much responsibility for their own washing as possible.

brushing teeth is fun for the children. Teach them to brush their teeth after eating, particularly after sweet or sticky snacks. Help the young children to squeeze an appropriate amount of toothpaste on the brush, show them the technique for brushing their teeth in the right direction, and then stand back and watch their pleasure. Give them the names that are associated with *teeth, gum, jaw, mouth, tongue, open, scrub, dentist.*

washing up can be a responsibility which the older children assume themselves. Part of the fun of playing in good clean dirt is the job of washing it off when you're finished playing. The school age girls and boys may become very interested in grooming, so manicure equipment, hair brushes and combs may be provided.

dressing and undressing are difficult

processes for the children to learn. You may be tempted to dress them yourself, since it's so much easier and quicker. However, if you do, you are taking from the child his chance to develop these skills for himself and become independent.

Older children can take the responsibility for deciding what clothes they will need to wear. Teach them how to dial the weather number, or to read a thermometer outside your window. Determine what reading on the thermometer will mean wearing a sweater, a coat and hat, and what conditions will call for boots and other protection. When the children are given this responsibility they do not whine, "Do I have to wear the coat?" or "I won't wear my hat."

Teaching children to dress themselves begins around two, for this is the age that most children are rather interested in the process of dressing, and are anxious to be as independent as possible. If you wait until later to let the child dress himself, until 3 or 4, he may be bored with the process, and would much rather let you continue to dress him.

You can help by breaking down the job of dressing into small segments, and by offering help with the difficult parts. You might help the child get into his jacket, and say, "Now you zip it up," or you might fasten all of the buttons on his sweater but the top two, leaving those for him. Give suggestions. When putting on shoes, for example, tell them to, "Put your toe in first," or "Hold your coat this way." Develop the idea that clothing helps to keep us well by protecting us from the weather, and by keeping us warm and comfortable.

an orderly environment "I have the kids pick up twice a day, once before nap, and again before going home."

A clean, orderly environment is necessary for healthful living. Children feel very grown-up when they have some responsibility for their day care home. They can be helped to pick up their toys, and taught the dangers of leaving a doll on the steps or a truck under the table. You can give them boxes to store their things in.

Children also feel good about themselves if you will let them help with the household chores. They can help you wash the plastic dishes, use a soapy sponge to wipe off the kitchen counter or table (a favorite activity) dust the bottom of things, or even to push the vacuum cleaner. Of course, you may have to go over things again later.

Mealtimes

Mealtimes are happy times in a home. Food nourishes a child's body, but it also seems to build in the child feelings of love, security and trust. Mealtimes give the children and the caregiver a time to share news, to gossip and giggle together.

The number and type of meals you serve will depend on the ages of the children, and the length of time they spend at the home. All meal planning should be done with knowledge of each individual child's eating patterns in mind. The parents and the family day care mother or father work closely together concerning the child's eating habits, his likes and dislikes and his growing, changing needs. The families' cultural or religious food preferences are respected and valued. You might ask the mother how to fix the 'greens' her children enjoy, how to make pinto beans as she does or for her recipe for the potato latkes their family enjoys at Hanukka.

Menus (including breakfast, a morning snack, a noon meal, an afternoon snack and in special instances, the evening meal) are planned with the proper balance of nutrients. Basically, children require the same nutrients as adults, although smaller quantities. Every day the meals and snacks should include foods from each of the basic four food groups: 1) milk and dairy products, 2) meats, fish and poultry, 3) vegetables and fruits, and 4) breads and cereals.

Children, with small stomachs, have small appetites. If presented with a large amount of food they quickly lose their appetites. On the other hand, if just a small portion of food is given, they feel it's manageable, realistic and appetizing.

It's nice to serve food in small bowls which the children can pass to one another, helping themselves to the portion they wish,

A Suggested Day
The times given are only approximate and will depend on the situation.

	Infants	Toddlers	Preschoolers	School Age
7 am	All children and their families are greeted warmly as they arrive. Many of the children will require some nourishment now, depending on their needs,			
	Babies may be changed, fed, and allowed to rest.	Some children may want to 'cat nap' or be rocked or cuddled for a while. Quiet toys—beads to string puzzles, dolls, books—can be available.		After eating, the children can read, finish homework, watch TV, or play a quiet game until time for school.
9 am	When the baby wakes, and feeding is completed, a game of peek-a-boo, or other play is enjoyed. Put the baby's seat or playpen near the activity of the children so he can watch.	Special Activities Art activities—painting, drawing, modeling, or other activity—cooking, playing with water or sand, making puppets, might be prepared for the children for in or outdoor play. A light snack is enjoyed midway through the morning.		
	Babies will probably require a full morning nap.	Many toddlers will require a full nap.	Preschoolers may need a quiet time to stretch out and rest.	
11 am	Some time for outdoor play—a walk around the block, to the store or playground—can be planned, following this period of active play, the children prepare for lunch by washing, helping with the food preparation or reading stories.			
Noon	Babies may be fed earlier, and may be ready for an afternoon nap.	Toddlers can learn to feed themselves.	Preschoolers can set the table, help to prepare the meal and help and clean up.	Lunch is ready for the children.
		After lunch help the children brush teeth and prepare for nap. Toddlers will probably require a full nap.	Preschoolers can brush their own teeth and prepare for rest. Many will nap, others will rest by playing quietly.	
1 pm	The children are allowed to sleep as long as they wish. Usually a refreshing drink or snack is welcome after napping.			
3 pm	Floor play—with baby placed on a blanket or in a playpen—can be planned	Active in and/or outdoor play follows nap. Some special activity, a game, story, or walk can be arranged.		A snack is ready for the children or they can fix their own. The children decide what to do with their time— building, sewing, painting, doing homework, going to clubs, listening to records, playing with friends.
5 pm	Preparing the children for going home helps them to make a smooth transition from your home to theirs. This is a good time for story reading, to gather together the things that each child will take home, or perhaps for a light snack to tide the children over until their parents prepare dinner.			

and always free to come back for seconds. As children serve themselves they develop feelings of self confidence and independence. Caring for their own needs, they gain dignity and self-worth.

Some children have peculiar likes and dislikes about food. Considering these preferences will help keep mealtime a happy, relaxed event. For instance, most children do not like foods all cooked together like stew, and sometimes they do not even like to have different foods touching on the plate.

Children seem to enjoy foods they can eat with their fingers. Raw vegetables, cut into bite sized pieces, are often substituted for cooked vegetables. Tossed salads may not be very popular, but serving the lettuce, tomatoes and carrots separately can make a big hit with the children.

Often how the food looks determines whether or not the children will like it. A variety of colors at each meal, along with a variety of textures is important.

Most important to successful mealtimes with children is the attention and company of the adults. The adult should try to eat with the children, and set the stage for a good, happy, relaxed time. Your eating habits and manners are copied by the children. You are the person who starts the table conversation, talking over the events of the morning with the children or whatever else that might interest them. Mealtime is a very important teaching time; use it well.

snacks

Sometime during the morning, and again in the afternoon, the children will want to eat. This snack doesn't need to disrupt their play, and can be a simple thing. Place a small pitcher of juice, some paper cups and a plate of crackers in the play area, and let the children help themselves to their snack.

School age children will be ready for refreshments when they return to the home in the afternoon. Something can be ready for them, or they may enjoy preparing their own snack.

Holidays, birthday parties and other festive occasions can be celebrated with a special snack, everyone sitting together in celebration of the occasion.

DEVELOPMENTAL ACTIVITIES FOR CHILDREN

Infants

Caring for a baby, watching him grow, is perhaps one of the most rewarding experiences a family day care parent can have. During the first year of life the infant is growing more rapidly than he will at any other time. He will be learning many things during his first year of life.

He will learn about himself . . . he will discover his hands, fingers and later his feet and toes . . . he will learn what he can make his body do . . . and that he is separate from his mother.

He will learn about the world . . . that the wind or air is cold on his face . . . the floor is hard and smooth . . . that he can make noise with pots and pans.

He will learn about others . . . that they respond to him . . . that he can make them laugh . . . that they care for him.

A baby learns with every experience. Everything is a teaching experience. When the baby is fed when he is hungry, changed when needed, he begins to learn that the world is a safe place, a secure place he can trust. If on the other hand, the infant's needs are never met when important to him, he begins to learn that the world is unsafe, a place he cannot trust or feel safe in.

Every time you cuddle the baby, hold him, fondle him, laugh, smile and talk to him, you are teaching. You, as the family day care parent, become a 'teacher' by giving the baby the experiences he needs to learn.

babies learn as they play

The young baby learns and plays by looking, listening and feeling. As he grows he tries out what can be done with almost any old thing—balls, little boxes, spools, spoons, metal dishes. These help the child develop a sense of know how, or competence—confidence in his ability to make something happen, to accomplish something—even something as simple as a new kind of sound.

. . . babies learn by looking

Give your baby something to see. Hang a mobile above his crib or:

- tie brightly colored magazine pictures, colorful scraps of material, old costume jewelry, or pieces of plastic straws to string and hang them from a clothes hanger.
- a shiny aluminum pie pan, a crushed ball of aluminum foil, or a brightly colored piece of tissue paper crumpled into a ball and hung where it can twist in the wind.

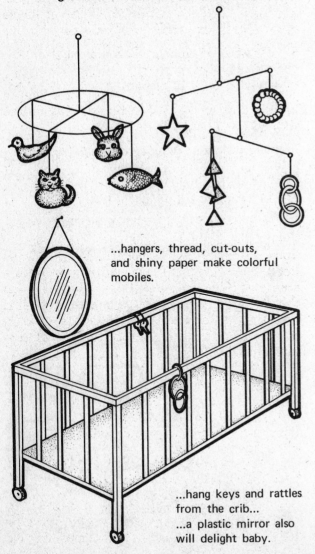

...hangers, thread, cut-outs, and shiny paper make colorful mobiles.

...hang keys and rattles from the crib...
...a plastic mirror also will delight baby.

- put some pictures on the walls of the nursery . . . tape some of the other children's art to the walls, mount some dried seed pods or flowers in an old box lid for the baby to see.

Although the very young baby will not be able to reach up and grab the mobile, you will want to be very certain that everything you tie to the hanger is securely and firmly attached and has no sharp, pointed edges.

One of the most interesting things for the baby to see is your face. Your face is important to the baby, it talks to him, smiles at him and laughs at him. When the baby smiles, your face smiles back, and when he gurgles and coos, you coo back at him. With these pleasurable experiences, the baby learns he is loved and enjoyed.

Have something for the baby to watch while you're changing or dressing him. A small mirror near his dressing table is fun for the baby to see himself in.

Sometimes you can play games with the baby, when he's in a playful mood, while you're changing him, or after he's been fed. Peek-a-boo and all of the old games you remember from your grandmother are fun for the baby, and very new to him.

All babies are different and each one will act in a different way. If he's smiling and watching you to see what will come next, he's most likely having fun and wants more. Follow the baby's cues and he will tell you what he likes and doesn't like. If the baby fusses or cries, or seems restless—he's had enough and it's time to stop.

. . . babies learn by listening

Every time the baby hears a sound, he's learning, and because he enjoys hearing new sounds and interesting things, he wants to learn more and more about his world.

- sing to the baby—even if you can't sing a note, the baby will be delighted and impressed with your ability as you sing nursery songs to him while you change or dress him.

- when the baby makes sounds, play with these sounds—when he makes a sound, a coo, gurgle or squeal—make it back to him. When he hears you repeating the sound he's made, he will make other sounds and soon you'll have a conversation going.
- rattle some plastic keys by the baby's ears, give him a safe rattle to hold on to.
- hang a set of Christmas bells or a wind-chime in the doorway, treating the baby to a new tune.
- take the baby with you around the house as you work or play with the other children. Let him see and hear the sounds of living —the whirl of the egg beater, the laughter of the children, the water rushing in the sink.

. . . babies learn by feeling

Around three months of age, the baby will be able to focus his eyes and will begin to use his hands to reach, touch and grasp the things he sees. From this point on, the baby will be very active, and will want many more things to play with. He needs toys he can feel—strings of plastic beads, rattles, floating bath toys or bells —toys he can shake, push, pull—toys he can finger, hold, touch and drop. As the baby feels, mouths, touches his toys he learns, and if he can make the toy do something he begins to learn that he is important in his world—he can make something happen.

- make a cradle gym—out of empty thread spools, plastic bracelets and other nice-to-pull objects, suspended securely on elastic across the crib . . . When the baby pulls the objects, the string stretches, and when he lets go, they bounce back.
- find playthings that are safe or different textures . . . find something that is soft, smooth, rough, bumpy or fuzzy.
- make a cloth ball by stuffing an old towel or scrap fabric with nylon stockings and sewing it together into a round shape.
- empty juice cans, with labels removed and no sharp edges, give the baby something smooth and rolling to play with.
- tie some netting together to form a puff ball, and watch the baby experiment as he plays with this 'prickly' toy.

The best thing that the baby can touch and feel is you. The warmth of your body as you hold him, your soft skin or dress, the rhythm of your body as you rock or walk, these are the things the baby needs to feel, and the things the baby learns from.

the older baby

When the baby can sit up he requires more challenging objects to play with. Now he can really handle an object, he can shake things, bang them, put them in his mouth, transfer them from one hand to another and even put one thing inside another.

Give him an empty box, and some object —a rattle, or plastic ball—hidden inside. Spoons to drop into a pan with a lid are fine too. The caregiver will need to supervise the baby closely, keeping bits of paper and other objects from his mouth, ears or nose.

Many household items are excellent toys for the older baby.
- nested cups of plastic
- measuring spoons on a ring
- wooden spoons
- boxes with lids
- old fashioned wooden clothespins
- pots and pans and lids
- empty band-aid cans
- a basket to put things in

MAKE YOUR OWN TOYS

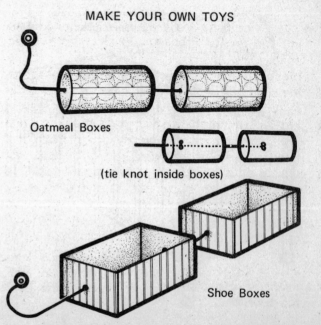

Oatmeal Boxes

(tie knot inside boxes)

Shoe Boxes

Clean and wash cans of
different sizes...
Remove sharp edges...
Decorate with paint or sticky paper...

Nest...

Stack...

Count...

All types of rolling toys, cans, oatmeal boxes, anything that can roll, are excellent for the baby, for they encourage him to creep after them. A set of blocks, a large cardboard box to crawl in and out of, a coffee pot, with glass parts removed, empty margarine and ice cream containers are all free, yet wonderful toys for the baby.

Some children become quite mobile during this first year of life. These children need spaces to explore safely, spaces to crawl and creep in. Playpens, although giving this scooting child a safe place, often limit his opportunity to actively explore his world. With careful watching the crawling baby should be allowed to move freely about a room, pulling himself up on stationary pieces of furniture, holding onto a wall or low table top as he tries out his legs. This intense time of motor activity—with the baby scooting and pulling into everything—demands that you child-proof your home. Cover electrical outlets, put lamp cords out of reach, and fasten rugs to the floor. Be certain to remove any small objects—pins, buttons, pieces of things, that might have accidentally found their way onto the floor.

. . . babies play outside

Babies enjoy going outside for some time every day. They enjoy watching the patterns of sun shining through the leaves of the trees, or when placed on a grassy spot of ground, they feel the prickly grass on their legs. A walk in the stroller, feeling the warm breeze and sun on their bodies, is a real experience for a baby.

When taking young babies out-of-doors, a stroller, carriage or infant seat is useful. Other times you may be able to lay a blanket on the ground and let the baby play on this, being careful of course, to watch to see that he cannot reach anything that might hurt him, or that nothing harmful can reach him, such as a passing dog or group of older children not aware of his presence.

If the baby has begun to crawl, you must be especially watchful. The opportunity for the baby to master the difficult skills of rolling over, crawling, pulling himself up to standing and walking can be safely practiced out-of-doors.

language activities

Of all of the skills the human infant learns, the ability to use language will be the most important for his future. To be able to use language, to speak, to write and to read, is the key to success at every level of life. The child entering grade school with the ability to listen and understand the spoken word, and the skill to express himself through words, is well on his way to achieving success in school.

Do infants have language? Ask any caregiver and she'll tell you, "Well, he surely makes himself understood." He cries in soft whimpers when he's wet, but you can always tell when he's hungry, for then he squeals and cries loudly." Babies do communicate, they cry, mew, gurgle, chuckle and produce a number of sounds. Babies listen to speech and are most responsive when they hear a human voice. A two or three-month old can be quieted, soothed or distracted with the sounds of his family day care mother's voice or the voice of his parents. By the second half of his first year he may understand his name, and the names of many things around him, and he may even begin to respond to the commands and verbalizations of the adults.

Every time you care for an infant—change a diaper, feed him, or wash him—talk to him, look at him, gain his attention by touching his arm or leg, and tell him "Now you're clean and dry," "just a minute and we'll get your bottle," "My how hungry you are." If the baby gurgles to you, gurgle and coo back. Repeating his sounds helps the infant begin to learn his language.

When the baby is older, use his name all of the time. Talk to him about the things you are doing. "Max is eating," "First put your leg here, and you'll be dressed." Before long, the child will begin to raise his arm when you say "Now your arm goes through this hole", or he'll wave 'bye bye' when someone he knows says 'goodbye', or he'll laugh excitely when you tell him "Your daddy is coming".

Sing nursery songs to the baby. Pat-a-cake may seem old hat to you, but to the eight-month old baby it's new and delightful. The rhythm, sound and pattern of the language found in nursery rhymes, plus the personal response the adult gives to the baby, help the baby to enjoy learning the sounds and patterns of his language.

Begin reading to the baby very early in his life. By four to six months of age you can hold the baby on your lap, and show him pictures in a magazine or book. The baby may pat the picture, gurgle and squeal over it. Show him picture books of animals, and make the sounds of the animals, naming them as you go along. The older baby will try to make sounds back to you. The holding, the sound of the human voice, and seeing the bright pictures in a book are all pleasurable and enjoyable for the child. Soon the baby will be able to point to the dog, rabbit or the baby when you ask, "Show me the . . ."

Make books for baby. Cut out bright pictures from magazines or catalogs, and paste these on cardboards from stocking packages or other clothing packages. Tie these together with a shoestring and you have a sturdy 'book' for baby. Put animal pictures in one book, flowers in another, food in one, and people in another.

Toddlers

When a baby begins to walk, usually around a year or so of age, until around the age of 3, he is often called a toddler—a baby, but now he's a walking baby. If all has gone well during the first year of his life, he now wants to be independent, and to do things for himself, pulling away from the adults around him.

The toddler wants to control his body—and he learns to walk, to climb, to run and jump. He wants to be master of his world—he would rather push his stroller than to ride in it and will struggle to get into his clothes and to button the buttons, rather than let someone do it for him.

Living with a toddler may be a real adventure. He's always on the go, always into things, trying to find out how they work. He enjoys being with other children, and learns from them. He watches others as they play, and sometimes enters into a joint activity for a few minutes, only to quarrel over some possession and run back to you for safety.

He doesn't wait well, and he needs a flexible routine, with plenty of freedom to have all of the activity he needs for his developing body. Because he needs to feel independent he may say "NO" to everything, trying to be less dependent on you than he was when he was a baby.

Toddlers like to feel they have helped with real household tasks, such as washing off a table after lunch or spreading their own peanut butter on their cracker or bread. It's good to find toys and things the toddler can play with that allow him to use them without your help or supervision.

Play is important to the toddler, for through play he will learn about the world, and himself. Concepts of rough and smooth, hard and soft, large and small develop as the children play with many different objects and things.

toddlers play

The walking baby, or toddler, needs toys and activities that give him new challenges. Toys that push and pull, strollers and carriages, things

56

that go up and down, that can be filled and dumped are appealing to him.

- They like to pull something in back of them. Oatmeal cartons, spools, shoeboxes, attached to strings or ropes are good pull toys.
- They like to put things inside of something and take them out. A set of nesting blocks can be made by washing and cleaning a series of three or four cans, removing sharp edges, covering them with shiny paper, and giving them to the children for stacking, nesting or rolling.
- They like to put clothes pins into a cardboard shoebox or tin can, and dump them out or to line them up around the edge of the box.

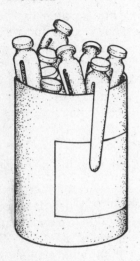

FOR TODDLERS

A smooth clean can and clothespins.

Though they're not nearly ready to master the skills of an adult, these children want to participate in adult life. They will delight in being able to handle soap, water, pots and pans and raw materials such as sand, leaves, or vegetables. The toddlers like to watch how things work, how people act, and how to play at being an adult.

- an old pocketbook filled with safe junk, some keys, nesting toys, small boxes, playing cards is enjoyed.
- a few old hats, a lunch box, tool kit, add to his playing at being grownup.
- a busy box, made by attaching a variety of hooks, locks, chains and bolts, and light switches to a board is fun to play with and to find out how things work.
- an old instrument panel, sometimes found in a Good Will Store, with switches to turn off

and on, and knobs to turn is fun. Be sure it is safe to use.
- let the toddler play in water, in the sink, tub or in a plastic pan, let him splash, pour, stir and experiment with water.

. . . play outdoors

Once the baby can walk, his world and his needs expand rapidly. Large muscle development demands that the toddler spend a lot of time out-of-doors. Give the walking baby some empty cardboard boxes to push around, to climb into or to put leaves in.

Very small piles of sand and dirt can be specially prepared for the children. A small sand shovel, plastic cups and other containers, plus your supervision, will keep the child happy, safe and busy exploring his world.

language activities

What a thrill when the child says his first word! Everyone is excited and impressed. His parents are overwhelming and the child is coaxed and cajoled into saying his 'word' for everyone who will listen. Some toddlers jabber all the time imitating the sounds around them, but use few real words.

Other toddlers will seldom speak, and then one day, suddenly begin using full sentences; still other children, who have seemed to enjoy talking, stop, using all their energies to learn to walk or run.

Usually the toddler uses one or two words in combination to mean many things. "Mommy up" may mean 'Mother is getting up,' 'I want to go,' or 'Pick me up.' The two words, "baby look" might be used to mean, 'give me a turn,' 'I see it,' or 'let me read the book.' In talking with children, you can expand on their sentences, saying back, "Oh yes, I see the dog, look he's barking at that boy," or "Yes, Jimmy is getting up, we'll go to the store" expanding these two word sentences into a longer, fuller sentence.

Help the children learn lanuage through listening:

- Ask them to listen to themselves . . . "Listen . . . how do your feet sound when you run on the grass?
- "Listen . . . how do your hands sound when

you clap them together?"
- "Listen . . . who is outside now?"
- Play some records for the children to listen to.
- Give them a string of bells to play with.
- Sing to them, "Skip, skip, skip to my Lou," as they hop around the room, or Hippety Hop to the Barber Shop.

Sitting very near to the toddler, or nestling him on your lap, read to him, every day, several times a day. These children will want to hold the book, and may, after they've heard you tell the story several times, 'read' it to you. *Saturday Walk* by E. Kunkle, *The Snowy Day* by Jack E. Keats, and the *Bundle Book* by Ruth Krauss are especially good for the child under three for they present factual information to him about the world in a very interesting manner.

Children under three do not realize the difference between what is real and what is pretend, and prefer books that explain their world to them in a truthful way. Remember, all the world is new and thrilling to the toddler. Stories cannot improve on real life. *Whistle for Willie,* by Keats, *Wait for William* and the *Angus* books by Marjorie Flack, *The Carrot Seed* and the *Growing Story* by Ruth Krauss, are all books that deal with events that toddlers are personally involved and interested in. Your librarian will be happy to help you find these and other good books.

Read a few favorite books over and over again to the toddler so he will come to know them as his friends. You might even make your own books for him, using pictures from magazines.

Make a book about his day and his life. Find pictures of children doing things such as brushing their teeth, eating or sleeping. Put these into booklets by pasting them on heavy paper or light cardboard. Write the story under the picture, using the child's name. Under a picture of a girl brushing her teeth you might write, "Jennifer brushes her teeth," and write the story of the child's day.

Sing more and more Mother Goose rhymes to the children. Jack be Nimble, Mary Had a Little Lamb, Little Miss Muffet, Little Jack Horner and many others. Repeat to him the Bo

Peeper and Pat-A-Cake from his younger days.

Encourage the child to begin to express himself with language. Show him pictures and ask him what he thinks is happening in the picture. He will begin talking about pictures by naming the things he sees. Ask him questions, What do you think will happen? What do you think has happened? What do you think will happen next?

Preschoolers

Growing in self-awareness, learning social skills, using language to make himself understood and to express his ideas, the preschooler is ready for many new experiences. Preschoolers enjoy and need to be with other children. They still may not be able to understand that other children have rights and wishes, so, they will need your supervision as they play.

The family day care home is a good place for preschoolers to play. Here they can, with a few close friends, act out the roles they may one day assume—playing "as if" they were the mother, the father or the teacher. Here they find carefully selected play materials and safe places to play.

You, the caregiver, do much to encourage and help the children in their play. You give them the materials and things to play with—finding things that provide them with a challenge, and putting away the toys they are no longer interested in. You also give them choices, knowing that they need to experience the results of making choices in order to learn how to make them. You let them decide what they want to play and how they want to play it. You might ask them, "Do you want to hear this story or read a poem? What should we do when we get to the park? Do you want to play with this box or these trucks? What should we do next?"

preschoolers play

Preschool children, the three, four and five year olds, find many things to play with. You will need to supply more complex and challenging things for them to use.

. . . make believe play

All young children need some time to

'make believe'. When children 'make believe,' they dress up and pretend to become the mother, father, doctor, bus driver or secretary. This play, rich with language, helps children to find out what it would be like to be the teacher, doctor or parent.

To help children with this play you will need some good strong, sturdy dolls. Boys, as well as girls, play with dolls. Large washable baby dolls are best, with a very few large doll clothes, or discarded baby clothes.

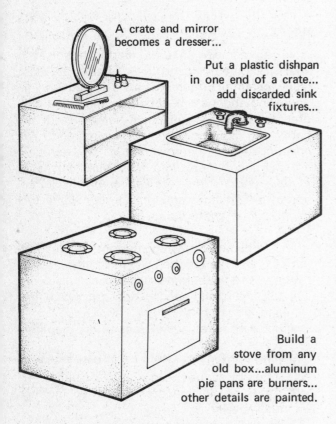

A crate and mirror becomes a dresser...

Put a plastic dishpan in one end of a crate... add discarded sink fixtures...

Build a stove from any old box...aluminum pie pans are burners... other details are painted.

Children love to play dressup. You can keep a dresser drawer of clothes for dressup play, or put some hooks inside a closet door to hang the clothes from. Children do not require elaborate dress materials. Give them:

- a piece of old lacy curtain for a King or Queen's gown;
- a lacy ladies half slip, with the elastic band tucked neatly under the children's arms for a fine costume for formal occasions;
- a variety of hats—ladies, firemen, workmen, service men to help the children act out people at work;
- discarded men's ties, an old jacket with

sleeves rolled up to add to play time.

- a purse or two, some old wallets, complete with toy money—or coupons cut from magazines, or poker chips to encourage the children to play 'shopping'.
- empty food boxes, empty and washed plastic milk cartons for a 'store' or 'kitchen'.

. . . manipulative play

All play involves the muscles of the children, and yet there is a type of play, known as manipulative, that encourages greater muscular coordination, and often involves the children in quiet, absorbing play of a repetitive quality. Bingo games, matching games, cards, table and sorting games and puzzles are all types of manipulative toys.

The child learns many skills by playing with these toys. He learns to see likenesses and differences, to count, and to observe shapes and colors closely.

puzzles

Puzzles are of great value to the child, for they ask him to look at shapes, colors and sizes, and to remember them. They must think a great deal when putting a puzzle together. The two- and three-year-old child can put simple puzzles together. You can make these puzzles from a piece of heavy cardbord. Take a large kitchen plate, draw a circle on the cardboard and cut it out. Then cut the circle into three or four pie-shaped pieces. Paint each piece another color. The children put these pieces back together to form a circle. A moon puzzle is made the same way . . . draw a circle on the cardboard, but cut this circle into arc shaped pieces.

CARDBOARD PUZZLES
Cut out shapes...color each piece differently.

For older children, any clear, colorful picture from a magazine can be mounted on a piece of cardboard. Rolling over the pasted picture with a rolling pin will help to take any wrinkles out of it. Cut the end result into different pieces, making more pieces for the older children.

Wooden puzzles can be purchased and are most desirable. These come in a variety of sizes and pieces. For older children you may even be able to find some cardboard puzzles that are appropriate.

flannel boards

Cover a piece of cardboard with material from some old flannel pajamas. Fill a box with shapes, pictures or letters, cut from cards, magazines or material. On the back of each of these shapes, glue a tiny piece of sandpaper, with the sandy side out. The sandpaper will make the shape stick to the flannel and the children arrange these anyway they wish. You might find an old story book that is too battered to use with the children. Cut the pictures from this book, put some sandpaper on the backs of them, and the children can tell the story by placing the cutouts on their flannel board.

matching games

Bingo games are matching games. The children must look carefully to see what things are alike. You can play bingo with commercial sets, or you can make your own. Pick up several stamp catalogs that are all alike from the supermarket, or ask your neighbors to save their copy of catalogs that come in the mail. Cut pictures that are alike from these catalogs, mounting them on pieces of cardboard. The older children then pick out the squares of cardboard that are the same. You might use scraps of wrapping paper to find several of the same pictures.

DOMINOES

Dominoes are one form of a matching game for the preschooler. Make a set of dominoes by painting cardboard or wood pieces. Make these larger than the dominoes you might buy in a toy store. Either paint dots on them, or buy transfer patterns to stick on.

Mount an old calendar on a shirt cardboard and cut it apart into numbers. Mount another calendar on another piece of cardboard. The children match the numerals on the calendar by covering them with the numerals on small squares.

sorting

Remember that wonderful button box your grandmother used to have with all those shiny, beautiful buttons? There's something very appealing about a box of buttons for young children, and the experience of sorting them according to size, shape and color is learning. *You must, however, be certain that the children cannot put the buttons into their ears, noses or mouths, and that they are kept safely away from any of the younger children in your home that might still be apt to do so.*

Put some empty egg cartons with the button box, and the children will have little trays in which to sort the buttons. Children can also sort:
- dry beans and seeds—popcorn, peas, lima and kidney beans
- different types and shapes of dry macaroni —shell, noodles, or alphabet
- different types of dry cereal that comes in different shapes—stars, circles, puffs
- a box of old beads or discarded earrings and jewelry
- old discarded nuts and bolts

stringing

Ask all of your friends to save you their empty spools. Give these to your children with long shoestrings to thread. Or give the children a dish of cheerios and some pipe cleaners. The children will eat, string and chat, enjoying this activity especially on a rainy day.

You can buy a box of wooden beads or find left over large beads from department store jewelry counters. These would have to be large enough to get a shoestring through easily.

. . . creative play

"Look what I made!" Everyone loves to make something and the young children in your care have special needs to 'make something'. When the children are allowed to work with art materials they learn to express their thoughts and ideas with symbols. They learn about colors and textures, sizes and shapes. A family day care home should have many choices of art materials for the children to use every day. Busy children, given many choices of creative activity, will have little time to get into trouble or mischief.

The children's art work may not look like much to you. At first the child just explores and experiments with the crayons on the paper, drawing lines any which way. He'll need large fat crayons that won't break in his tightly clenched fist, and large sheets of paper. If you can't find a printing shop near by that will give you scrap paper, you can save old grocery bags, and by cutting them open have plenty of paper for the children to draw on. You may want to be sure that the children are drawing on a washable surface, for when first learning, they often make marks off of their paper. These first drawings will not mean too much to the child. They've been done haphazardly, and the doing is the fun.

Eventually the child will learn to control his scribbles and you will begin to notice shapes in the drawings. He will make circles and ovals, and be able to repeat these shapes. One day he may begin to name his circle . . . calling it a man, or a bird, and he'll put other shapes together to make a house or a car. Don't expect to be able to actually see a 'man' in the child's drawing, his art will not be realistic for several more years. The young child, some people believe, draws what he knows and feels. He may draw his father with very long legs and a tiny head, for to the child, always looking up at this tall person, his father may appear to be mostly legs.

Sometimes it's hard to know what to say to a child about his scribbles. The children will be hurt if you ask them "what is it?", or confused if they really haven't thought or cared about what it could be. If you say to them, as they scribble, "that looks like a dog, is it a dog?" when they were really thinking of an airplane, or

just trying to gain control of the crayon, their eyes and muscles, they'll become discouraged, and will not enjoy drawing.

You can, however, show the children you are interested in their work, by asking them to tell you about their drawing, or by commenting on how hard they worked, or how many bright cheerful colors they have used.

do not give children coloring books

These books say to the child that 'this is the only way to draw.' They teach children to believe that they can't draw because they could never make a picture of a dog as well as the one in the coloring book. It's also very important for children to learn to think, to use their own ideas. Giving them a book, with pictures some adult has thought about and made, takes away the opportunity for them to think for themselves.

Start off gradually, giving the children crayon and paper, dough, paste and scissors, as their first art materials. Later, after both you and the children feel comfortable with art work, add other more messy activities.

language activities

Flowering with language, the preschool child talks, listens and understands. Read a story to him every morning and every afternoon. Find some special place in your house or apartment —it may be the sofa in your living room, a special chair, the front steps, your front porch, under a tree or in the backyard. Call this place your "story chair," or "the story steps," and keep it reserved for a special place to read and tell stories.

As you read the story to the preschoolers, let them see the pictures, and let them talk about the story as you read it. After you have read the story, ask them to talk about the parts they liked best, the pictures they liked, or the parts that may have frightened them.

Have the children bring their own personal response to the story. Help them to act it out. If you have read the story of the Three Billie Goats Gruff, ask them to pick the person or animal they would like to be and have them act out the story, ask them to say the words the billy goats said. You don't need any costumes to act out stories, and you can pretend a bridge by putting a chair on its side. Ask them to read to you by interpreting the pictures.

MAKE A PUPPET STAGE

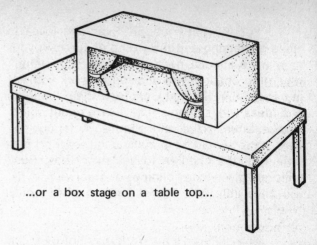

...or a box stage on a table top...

...turn a table on end

Hold a puppet show. Take an old rubber ball, poke and pull a hole in it, and let the children decorate the ball with eyes, hair, a mouth and ears. Put the ball on their finger, and they have a 'finger puppet'.

Take a small paper bag, put your hand inside it, and move the folded bottom up and down to get the idea of a mouth . . . decorate the bag with suggestions of a story character. Do you have a worn out sock without a partner? Put your hand all the way in the sock, and tuck a mouth in between your fingers and thumb; glue on button eyes, some hair, a mouth and add other decorations and you have another puppet. Or simply let the children draw a character from a story on a piece of paper, mount the entire sheet on a piece of light weight cardboard, cut the figure out and paste it on a stick and you have a stick puppet.

ALL KINDS OF PUPPETS

...use a tall chair

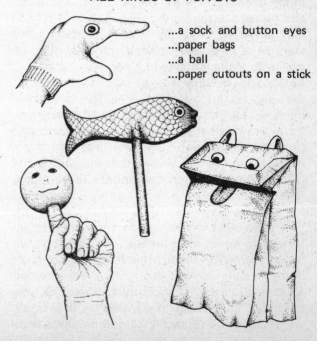

...a sock and button eyes
...paper bags
...a ball
...paper cutouts on a stick

. . . language games

You talk to the children all day, they talk to you, they listen to the radio, television or records, they hear the sounds of the street, and the sounds of the park. There is really no time of the day that the children are not learning language in your home. Sometimes, with the older children, your preschoolers, and even your school age children, you can play some fun games with language. Suggest to them when they say to you "what can I do" or let the school children teach them and play with the younger ones when they get home from school. You will make up your own games, here are some suggestions that mothers have enjoyed with children of many ages.

- See if the children can play the "Opposites Game." You think of a word, and the child tells you the opposite word. You may begin by saying Hot, and the child would say Cold. Other words are up, down, light, dark, sweet, sour, soft, hard, slow, fast, in, out and so on. Let the children take turns at leading this game.
- On another day play the "Riddle Game" with the children. This game helps the children to use and understand language, and fosters the use of descriptive words. The mother looks around the room and sees an object. She says to the children "I see something blue. Guess what I see?" And the children try to guess what she is thinking of. Now the children take turns, selecting some other object to describe to the day care mother and their friends.
- Play a "Silly Game" on a hot afternoon when there's nothing to do. Give the children a silly direction. Tell them, "Touch your hair, then touch your toes." See if they can remember the things you've told them to do. When they can carry out one direction, add another. Three directions in a row is enough for even a five year old to remember. After they have had a turn, it's time for you to listen and follow their directions. This game helps them to listen to, and interpret language, and helps them to remember things.

THE SCHOOL AGE CHILD IN FAMILY DAY CARE

"Hey, I'm home from school" shouts the child, and you are there to greet him with a hug or smile. Just as his mother or father would, you take the time to listen to the child, to ask him how his day was, to talk about his schoolwork, and to show him that he is loved and accepted in your home.

The older child still needs some place to go and someone to watch out for him until his parents come home from work. He can find the family day care home a welcome place. Here he can be the big brother or sister to the younger children, or to his own siblings, he can read to them, demonstrate his new skills and abilities, and generally take the role of the older, more knowledgeable authority.

Just as the school child would have a great deal of freedom within his own home, he can also have it in the family day care home. He can have the freedom to select his own activities, he can decide which clubs he will belong to, who he will play with and what he will do. Yet the child is not entirely on his own. You know you are responsible for the child, and he will know that you need to know where he will be. You as his caregiver, continue to be concerned about him, and, more importantly, are there when he needs you.

FREE TIME

All children need free time, but the school child, who has had a host of well meaning adults telling him all day where to go, what to do, what to think and how to behave, must find the time in the home to relax, to think for himself, to be himself and to find himself. He's free in the home to do nothing, or free to do something. He's free to do something with someone else or free to do it by himself.

Perhaps you can arrange for the child to find some spot in your home or apartment, away from the other children, that he can call his own. Whatever your arrangement, the school child will need some materials, games and books to use as he chooses.

Creative Materials

Even if your children attend an art club in the neighborhood or take part in a crafts program at the recreation center, you will still want to have available for them a wide variety of creative materials. The school child can use all of the art materials you've provided for the younger children, but they will use them in a different way. Now the child is increasingly anxious to produce a product with his work, something that is real, that can actually be used, or framed or hung in his room at his home or in yours. The children will enjoy:

- a sewing box, with scraps of materials, needles, thread, buttons to make puppets, purses, or actual pieces of clothing for dolls or themselves.
- larger pieces of felt or burlap to embroider designs or to make a wall hanging.
- a kit to make pot holders with.
- model cars, boats, airplanes to put together.
- a box of junk—small boxes, pieces of wood, styrofoam, strong glue and masking tape to build things with.
- scraps of soft wood, hammer and nails, and a place set aside for woodworking—an old table top, outdoors or in the basement, and a clamp are all that is necessary.
- paints, chalk, crayons and paper, clay and modeling materials plus some cardboard scraps to mount their drawings and paintings on, or construction paper they can use to frame their work.

Science

Science activities are fascinating to the child and a number of them can be offered in your home.

- Let the children help you plant seeds in your yard, or if you live in a city and have no yard, you can plant seeds in discarded milk cartons and enjoy watching things grow.
- Plant a handful of grass seeds on a wet sponge, or a piece of dampened paper toweling.
- Experiment with planting seeds, plant some seeds in different containers, using different types of soil, and different watering schedules to see which seeds will sprout first, and which plants will grow the fastest.
- Plant all of the seeds you and the children find in food—apple seeds, orange and grapefruit seeds, tomato and green pepper seeds.
- As you prepare for dinner, cut the tops from turnips, carrots, beets or radishes leaving

about ¼ inch of the vegetable. The tops of these root vegetables, when placed in a shallow dish of moist gravel or water, will soon grow into ferny plants.
- Plant a white potato or a sweet potato in a glass of water and watch it grow.
- A terrarium can be planted in an old mayonnaise jar. Put a piece of charcoal in the bottom of the jar to prevent spoilage, and a layer of gravel for drainage, followed by a layer of dirt. Find some small plants in the park, around your building or use some seeds to plant inside the jar. Water your jar once, close the lid. The terrarium should never need watering again.

Children enjoy caring for pets, and watching living things. You do not need to live in the country to give your children the experience of caring for living things.
- Fish, gerbils, or guinea pigs are clean, take little room, and are easy to care for.
- Fill a jar with some dirt and a handful of ants. Put a drop of water in the jar, some food crumbs, and close the lid tightly. Cover the outside of the jar with dark paper. When you remove the paper in a few days, the children will be able to see the tunnels and homes of the ants.
- Help the children to observe the living things around them, watching the pigeons, squirrels, starlings and sparrows. String popcorn and cranberries to hang outside your window or on your balcony and count the number of birds that come to feed on a winter's day.

The weather can be used to help children learn scientific concepts, and is always available for their explorations.
- Collect snow in a cup, bring it inside and watch it melt.
- Put a cup of water on the outside of the window sill, and see how long it will take to turn into ice.
- Hang a thermometer outside of the window. The children can chart the temperature changes. Let the children bring the outdoor thermometer inside—put it in a glass of water, have the children place both hands around the glass to see if the heat of their hands causes the temperature to rise. Put the thermometer in a pan of luke warm

water, ice water and warm water. What happens?

- Judge how hard the wind is blowing by feeling the wind, watching a flag, or taking a pinwheel outside.

Other Materials

Table games, monopoly, bingo, checkers, jigsaw puzzles and cards might be enjoyed by a group of school age children. They'll enjoy playing a game with you. Older children still learn as they engage in make-believe play. Their play becomes more organized. They want to put on real plays before audiences, and take part in designing and making sets and costumes. Doll play, with cowboy, soldier, and teen age dolls, is popular.

Collections

Who knows why the school age child loves to collect things? Some people say it's because he now feels that he must become the master of something, or that now he's in school he feels he must do things in a regulated fashion. Whatever the reason, the school age child often has a hobby. The family day care parent can find out what his interest is, and build on this. He may be interested in stamps, and you can save the unusual stamps you find on your mail, or he may be collecting playing cards, or pictures of horses, or rocks. Recognize his hobby by adding to his collection, and giving him a place to keep it. Saving an egg carton for his rocks, or an empty kleenex box for his stamps, shows him that you respect his hobby.

Community Groups or Clubs

Clubs, both formal and the informal secret type, are of great interest to the school age child. Just because children are enrolled in a family day care home is no reason for them to miss out on the Brownie, Cub, Boy or Girl Scouts, 4-H, Campfire Girls, or other formal clubs if they want to join and if their parents agree. These children need the feelings of belonging to something, and should have all of the opportunities for club life that the community offers. Some community clubs are:

- School clubs—the school itself may sponsor a recreation program, art or music or drama club after school.
- Recreation and parks programs—the recreation department may have organized sports, craft, dancing or homemaking clubs.
- Churches—local churches may sponsor after school activity programs for children.
- Community centers—the community center may offer ceramics, painting, or sports clubs.

The wider community should be available to the school age child. All children need opportunities to find out about their wider world. You can arrange for:

- a trip to the library to help the children obtain a library card if they don't already have one.
- a visit to other community services, the fire, police and sanitation department in the neighborhood.
- a walk around the neighborhood or to the local shopping area.

Physical Play

School age children, who may have been sitting for long periods of the day, will need some free time for physical activity. Check to see if there are sports activities or teams the child would like to join through the school, the neighborhood playground, the community center or the YMCA.

Group activities and sports do not appeal to all children, but it is important for you to help those children who desire them to have the opportunity, and to expose the other children to the opportunity. Even if an organized group is present in your neighborhood, you may want to supplement this physical activity with additional outdoor play.

Provide the children with several different types of balls—baseballs, basketballs, tennis or volley balls—jump ropes, or hoops for outdoor play. They can use these by themselves or together with a neighbor or friend.

When they have the space and freedom to dig, and some scrap lumber, school age children may like to construct a huge fort-like structure. Sometimes they can build in a back yard, an empty neighborhood lot, or the schoolyards. Some communities in big cities have arranged for small 'vest pocket' parks for the children to build in.

Army surplus stores often have heavy cargo nets that you might be able to hang from a fence or a tree for the children's climbing activity. Rope swings are popular, and old tires for them to roll and build with are useful, if you have outdoor spaces for children's play.

Most of all, the school child needs the opportunity to run, jump, climb, and yell. If this is not possible in your building's recreation area, or in your immediate neighborhood, then you may be able to arrange for the children to use the nearest playground, park, or recreation center.

EDUCATION ACTIVITIES

A mother teaches her children, and helps them with their school work. As a caregiver, one of your responsibilities is to give the children the kind of home-like atmosphere that makes it possible for them to succeed in school. This does not say that you have responsibility for helping them with homework and other school involvement, but it does mean that you can supplement their home in this area.

Attitudes About School

"Why must I go to school?" This is a question that every child asks at one time or another, either out loud or to himself. The sooner the child learns that he needs the basic skills of reading, writing, listening, speaking, the easier it will be for him to accept help in learning them. He must have these basics to learn marketable skills. He must be able to read if he is going to be a race car driver, a football player, a fireman or parent. Thus it is very important for you to help him to build good feelings about school.

Activities

You should find out from the child's mother or father whether or not you can help in school related activities. Remember to plan with the mother. She may not have enough time to do all of the things that she wants to do concerning school. It is good for the child's teacher to know that you are with the child a good portion of the day. In that way, if there is extra homework to do, or a meeting for you to attend, she may be able to contact you. She may also ask your help on a school trip. Perhaps she will let you take the young children with you. These trips can be fun for everyone.

Homework

Show interest in the child's homework and help him when you can. Helping a child with his homework is not wrong as some people may think. What can be wrong with helping with homework is when you do it FOR the child and not WITH him. Remember that follow-up about homework is important too. Find out how his teacher liked his work. Compliment him when the work is good, encourage him to make it better. Remember that honesty with children is very important. Some of us just can't do that 'new' math or advanced social studies so be honest with the child when you really don't know the answers. Try to find the answers, but don't be afraid to let him know that there are some things that you don't know. It will help him to understand that you are human, that everyone can't know everything, and that each of us has his strengths. Trade places with him, when he understands something that you do not: let him teach you. That age old question "what did you learn in school today?" is a loving question, keep asking it until the answer changes from nothing to something. Your interest and understanding of his work in school will help him with his self-esteem and it will help your relationship.

Reading

Sometimes children need help in learning the basic skills of reading. You might be able to help them, if you can do so without pressuring the child, without becoming upset, or upsetting him. You might ask the child's parents or teachers for games he can play at home, or the librarian can help you select books that he could read in your home.

Many other things help a child with reading, perhaps even more than trying to help him directly. You can set aside some time every day to read to the older children.
- Read a chapter, or a part of a chapter, (condensing it) from *Call of the Wild, Sounder,* or some other classic each afternoon.
- Find books from the library that the children may be able to read by themselves, or with some help from you, *Two is a Team,* or *Roosevelt Grady* could be enjoyed with you

reading a section out loud and the children reading another part.

- Use newspapers and current news magazines with the children. Point out to them, or read to them, stories that are of interest —the new pandas, the boy who saved a dog, or the story of the largest pumpkin.
- Encourage children to make their own books. Give them several sheets of paper stapled or sewed together. Label these books, "What I like Most," "How I Felt When I Was Sick," "My School Book," "Things I Wear," "Things I Do Not Like." The children draw or cut out pictures illustrating these topics, and you can write down their stories as they tell you about them. The older children will want to write their own words under the pictures.
- Let the children write notes to their parents. If a child comes home from school upset by some incident, or excited about some accomplishment, ask him if he would like to dictate it to you so you can write it down for his parents.

These activities encourage and stimulate the children to read and write for themselves, and demonstrate fully the usefulness of the spoken and written language.

SUMMER ACTIVITIES

During the summer, the school children may be with you every day, all day. Keep plenty of creative materials on hand, lots of playmates, and things for them to play with.

To keep the school child busy all summer, have them:
- Make some puppets and put on a puppet show for the neighbors.
- Freeze cool aid or concentrated orange juice or yogurt in paper cups, putting a plastic spoon in each cup before it becomes firm . . . eat like popsicles.
- Make jello to eat.
- Make peanut butter and jelly sandwiches and go to the park.
- Find an ant hill and collect the ants in a jar.
- Put a blanket over a clothesline and play fort.
- Teach them to play "Cootie," "Tic Tac Toe," or "Hang Man."
- Turn the sprinkler on and play in the hose.

- Put six unrelated things in a paper bag, a feather, a hat, ring, or anything and tell the children to make up a play about them and give it for you.
- Go fishing.
- Give them a dry cell battery, a flashlight bulb and some coated wire: how long will it take them to light the bulb?
- Walk in the rain.
- Give them a stack of magazines, some papers stapled together and have them make scrapbooks.
- Get a stack of cardboard boxes and some paint and brushes, let them paint to their hearts' content.
- Play summer Olympics . . . who can bounce a ball the longest, jump the farthest, hop the highest, hop the longest?
- Take a magnifying glass outside.
- Make a "Pick a Treat" jar . . . in the jar are slips of paper with all types of treats such as "one free popsicle," "you do not have to clean up today," "take your lunch anywhere you want," "pick a cookie," "one turn with the view master," written on them.
- Bake a cake and have a Fourth of July, Happy Birthday America party.
- Fill an empty coffee can with water and take a brush and paint the sidewalks.
- Go to the library for story hour.

DISCIPLINE AND THE SCHOOL AGE CHILD

Self-Esteem

Two important aspects of dealing with the school age child are self-esteem and trust. The more time, effort and patience that you devote to these two things, the easier it will be for you to have discipline. You must build up the self-esteem of the child. When a child thinks well of himself he will be much easier for you to discipline. You must show him that you trust him, you must show him that he is important to you. When he begins to understand that you trust him, when he begins to understand that you feel that he is very important, then with this mutual understanding the problems that usually occur with discipline will disappear. Self-esteem and trust mean good discipline.

Be positive. Use the strengths of each child. The more you value the child, the more he will value himself. Use his strengths and talents to make him look at himself in a good way. Let the child know by example and attitude that it is all right to express his feelings, both good and bad. Let him know that it is all right to show love, enthusiasm, sympathy, loneliness, frustration, pain and even anger. But, tell him that there is a time, a place and a way to show these feelings without hurting himself or other people. You have a very important role.

Trust

The child must trust you. You have to demonstrate by what you say and do that you can be trusted. In this way, you build trust in the child and work toward making this trust mutual.

You can make reasonable rules and regulations. If you make sure that the child understands them, that he has a chance to help you make these rules, then you will have better discipline. For example, when he knows why there are rules, and when he understands that the rules will not change from situation to situation, discipline is easier.

Make a list and put it on the wall. For the older child it is more important for him to know that all rules are fair. When you have older children you will never be able to be with them every minute. As you well know, they are probably able to "beat the system" a million ways. You trust *them*. Take for example, the playground. The playground may be a block away and you can't see it from your house. If you have a nine-year-old boy, you would not want to sit and watch him every minute of the afternoon as though he were a five-year-old, and he would hate the whole idea of you babysitting for him. So you establish trust as a two-way street. When he obeys the rules you will trust him. Write down your do's and don'ts for the playground for the first day.

For example:

- Do stay on the playground, not in the alley or the street.
- Do play with boys your own age, stay away from the bullies.
- Do treat the little boys nicely, don't tease them, etc.

The first few days you go to the play-ground with the boy. The next few days only stay half the time, the next few days stay only a few minutes to see what the situation is like. Then don't go at all. Do everything you can to build up trust between you and the child. Help him to trust you. Learn to trust him. Self-esteem and trust is what discipline is all about.

Responsibility

A good way to attain discipline is to give responsibility to the child. It will also give him more self-esteem.

There are many ways to give the child responsibility other than allowing him to take care of younger children. For example: shopping. One day a week you could have him go shopping with you, not only to help carry the bags, but so that he can learn about prices, values of food money, and how to measure contents or weight of food. This is another example of using every-day chores as a learning experience. If his parents agree, and assume liability, it might be nice if he could find some older person who lives near you and go shopping with, or for them once a week. He might get some small tip or pay from the older person and a relationship with a senior citizen can be a very good experience for a child who may not have older relations living near him. Another responsibility that you can give to your child is to keep his own play and work area clean, or to help you with the dishes after you both have had a meal.

Talking About Problems

A caregiver develops a sense of trust with her children, and builds a close feeling of mutual respect. She is there and able to talk to the children when they have questions to ask her. They may want to know what's it like to grow up, to have a baby, or they may be worried over some type of misinformation an older child at school has told them about sex. It may also be that they have been exposed to drugs, or have seen other children at school using drugs, smoking or drinking alcohol and they are concerned about what to do.

There really isn't anything so dreadful that you, as the child's caregiver, cannot talk to him about it. Just as his mother and father will discuss his questions with him when they return from work, you can talk to him about his concerns as they arise. It is important though, that there be complete agreement between you and the child's parents on these issues, that you talk to the parents about your discussion.

sex education

In a family home, children naturally become aware of differences between boys and girls, and of some of the facts of reproduction. As the children become older, they may need additional information about sex. The child's parents will want to give this information, but you may be able to answer the child's questions as they arise. Discuss with the parents, beforehand, the points they feel you can discuss with their children.

Try to find out what the child is really asking you, and then answer him as honestly and frankly as you can. If you can't talk about some things without being embarrassed, ask his parents to answer these things. Often if you ask the child what he thinks the answer is to his question, you'll get some good clues as to what he is really asking you, and how you can help him.

drugs

Attitudes toward drugs are taught as you live together, just as attitudes about sex are taught through the natural day-to-day living. The proper use of medication should always be stressed in your home. You do not misuse even simple things like aspirin, cough syrups, or throat lozenges.

Sometimes you and the children may get into deep discussions about the use of drugs. You will want to obtain the parents' consent before entering into these discussions, and then inform the parents about them. The local welfare and health agencies, as well as Federal agencies, may have information and printed pamphlets that will help you to know the facts about drugs. With these materials and other resources from the agencies in your neighborhood, you can help the children sort out the facts for themselves, and reach sensible conclusions.

Remember too, that a child who feels accepted, secure and is full of confidence in himself and in his ability to decide for himself, will be that child who will *not* feel the need to try drugs or to "go along with the gang."

Peer pressure may be great, but a child who has all of the security he needs, within your home and his own, will not have to try out something to feel important, to get attention or to be part of a group.

MORE ACTIVITIES FOR CHILDREN OF ANY AGE

INDOOR PLAY ACTIVITIES

Creative Play

drawing

Large crayons of many colors, and many different types of paper should always be available for the children. They can draw on:

- Cardboard sheets that come in stocking, shirt and underwear packages.
- The want ad section of the newspaper.
- The backs and insides of old greeting cards.
- The inside of a box lid.
- A styrofoam meat tray.
- Scraps of material.
- Wood scraps.

Children can draw with:

- Crayons
- Colored chalk. If you spray the drawing with hair spray or spray starch the chalk dust won't rub off.
- Water color marking pens. Protect the table top with newspaper, for these pens sometimes 'bleed' through the paper.

modeling

Push, pulling, squeezing, patting and pounding—children enjoy modeling. Every home needs something for the children to model with.

. . . salt dough

3 to 4 parts of flour
1 part of salt
water to mix into a dough
a drop of food coloring if desired

This dough will dry, and the children can 'save' their products. If you want to keep it for a longer time, add a teaspoon of cooking oil, and you can use it over and over again. Dough can be stored in the refrigerator.

. . . commercial clay

Commercial Clay—You can purchase clay from an art supply store. It will never wear out. The children can model with it, and if they make something, it will harden and they can take it home. If they don't want to keep their product, you can crumble it up and add some water to it, and it returns to its moist state. Keep the clay in an old plastic diaper pail or plastic bag.

. . . other doughs

Other Doughs—Think of the other things children can model with. A piece of bread dough can be poked and molded and then baked in the oven. When you open up a can of biscuits, give the child one to play with, and when you're baking cookies, let him have some of the dough to shape.

When modeling, give the children a piece of oilcloth, shiny side down, to work on. Newspapers will not protect a table top from modeling clay, and a piece of plastic is too slick to work on. Children can learn to clean up after themselves, and to sweep up any pieces of clay that have fallen on the floor.

cut and paste

Another activity children enjoy is cutting and pasting. You can buy small scissors for the children to use, and many different types of paste.
- Liquid paste that comes in small bottles with a squeeze top.
- White solid library paste is handy to store in small containers, and can easily be spread by the children.
- Strong, white liquid glue is excellent, for it adheres to nearly any surface.
- You can make paste by mixing flour and water until you get the consistency you desire.

You can store your paste in empty cans or margarine tubs. Give the children tongue depressors, or let them use their fingers to spread the paste. You can also put liquid paste in squeeze bottles (detergent or baby lotion bottles) and the children can squeeze out just the amount they need.

Children can paste things on:
- box lids
- lids from egg cartons
- brown paper bags cut open
- any kind of paper
- meat trays
- discarded wrapping papers

Children can paste:
- strips and pieces of bright colors cut from magazine pictures
- pieces of scrap wood
- paper doilies, fancy papers from food packages
- scraps of string, yarn, ribbons
- dried leaves or seed pods
- parts of greeting cards
- pieces of scrap material
- pictures from seed, toy, clothing catalogs
- bits of cellophane, straws, and other fancy paper
- feathers

First experiences with cut and paste are collages in which the child pastes an assortment of things on his paper. Children are first happy with one or two things pasted on the paper. Sometimes, children first learning to paste will place things right on top of one another. Soon, however, they enjoy arranging the materials to form a design or picture.

painting

All children love to paint, and you can let the children paint in your home. You can use a table top, the floor, or the wall for your easel. Cover all surfaces with an old plastic shower curtain or other water proof material. You can purchase tempera paints in a dime store, or you can make your own paints.

Here is a recipe for making homemade paint:

1 cup liquid starch
6 cups of water
½ cup soap powder
Dissolve soap in water and mix well with starch. Add food coloring of your choice.

You will have to supervise children with this paint. You may find that it is easier to purchase powdered or prepared tempera paint at the dime store or art supply store. The children can paint with any kind of brush—a paint brush purchased at the hardware store, an old pastry brush, or regular brushes designed for young children.

Put your paint in an empty juice can, and store the cans in a cardboard soft drink six pack container. These can be carried wherever they will be needed, and the container keeps them from spilling. Keep one can of water in the container, for rinsing or cleaning the paint brushes. When you finish with the paints, fix a 'lid' of aluminum foil and a rubber band for each can. Margarine tubs with their tight fitting covers keep prepared tempera paints from drying out between use.

Anything can be painted. Children can paint:

- cardboard boxes
- egg cartons
- paper tubes from wrapping, toilet or wax paper
- paper bags
- paper plates

If you are not sure of yourself or the children, start by giving the children one color of paint, and add other colors later. The children can help you with the clean up, carrying the brushes to the sink, washing off the table with a soapy sponge.

junk construction

Along with the paste, give the children some masking tape and a collection of empty boxes, rolls from toilet paper and wrapping paper, the dividers from cookie and candy packages, and any other interesting bits and pieces of things. The styrofoam that comes in many packages, film cartridges, bits and pieces of wood can also be used. From this 'junk' box, the children select the materials they need to make something. The masking tape holds the empty cans or boxes together for the children to build a castle, rocket ship or just a fantastic creation.

blocks

All children love to build with blocks. Wooden unit blocks can be found in toy stores and, although they are expensive, they will last forever. A starter set of about 100 blocks is usually around $15. A group of four children will require at least 200 blocks to build with.

If you cannot affort wooden blocks, you can make substitute blocks for the children. Take cardboard milk cartons and open them up. Stuff them solidly with crumbled newspapers and close the top, flattening it out, sealing it with tape. You can have a variety of sizes of cartons from the pint containers to the large gallon sizes. If you find the printing on the outside of these distracting, you can cover them with sticky plastic paper to give you a set of blocks all the same color.

...wash and open...stuff with paper...close and seal...

MILK CARTON BLOCKS

...cover with sticky-back paper...use all sizes.

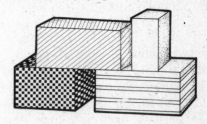

Tape the lids shut on cigar boxes or shoeboxes for a different type of block. The shoeboxes should also be stuffed solidly with paper to give them more sturdiness. Let the children build with blocks of a different kind. Give them full cans and boxes of mixes from the kitchen shelf to build with. When the boxes begin to show signs of wearing out, you can use them.

Perhaps you will be lucky enough to know a carpenter or live near a cabinet shop or lumber yard. These places will be happy to give you their left over wood scraps, which, when sanded, are excellent blocks for children.

Television

"But what did you watch before you had TV?" asked the little girl. To the young child, TV is a common part of his life and he cannot imagine the time when people did not have access to its wonders. Children accept TV as a normal part of their life, but a part that holds tremendous fascination for them, and has become a major source of recreation.

Children spend many hours watching television, and there are many shows that can be stimulating and informative for them. These shows introduce him to other people and new ideas, and give him feelings of other places. Not all shows are of value, or even desirable for children, however.

For the child under three, very few TV shows are appropriate, and these children should not spend their time watching television. Young children appear to be interested mostly in the changing random light patterns, and the movement they see, rather than any story plot. The young child, confused about fact and fancy, cannot tell when something has actually happened and when it is just pretend. He may become very frightened when he sees the cartoon monster eating an airplane or chasing a child. The same thing could happen to him; after all, he did see it, didn't he? So it must be true.

Older children may find TV an escape from real life, and it may keep them from learning to play with others. Children who are fearful, who are having trouble in school, or wondering why their parents have left them, may find escape in TV.

Then too, many shows on TV are questionable in content. Some shows poke fun at the man with a big nose, or a limp—seeming to teach the children to laugh at people who are different. Other cartoon shows, consisting of the endless hit and chase scene, offer the children nothing of interest and little of value. If you as a

family day care parent really want to help the children in your care to grow and become productive, intelligent, loving people, then you should take the time to assist them in their television viewing.

be selective

First of all, you must remember that televisions do come equipped with a plug that you can pull, and a knob that can turn the set off and on. You can decide when and what you and the children will watch. Take the time to help the children select the shows that are worthwhile and that offer them real enjoyment, pleasure and knowledge. Some TV shows that children continue to enjoy are Captain Kangaroo, Mr. Roger's Neighborhood, Me Too Shows, the Ripples Series, Sesame Street, Electric Company, and the Friendly Giant. Other shows of value may be found by checking your local listing on the educational channel. Having the children select their own show from a list you give them can make this task easier.

keep the children busy

When you have plenty of choices for the children to make, things for them to do, art materials to work and create with, books to read and places to go, they will often find television rather boring. When children are able to work with their hands, to play with one another, they will only want to watch a special show occasionally, and will not find the passive experience of sitting in front of a set very exciting or stimulating.

involve the children

When you and the children watch a show together, you can help provide some personal involvement to make the viewing more meaningful. When you watch with the children you can discuss the show with them . . . asking them what parts they thought were funny and why, and help them to work through those parts they found confusing or didn't understand or which frightened them.

Find some object or thing that the show introduced for the children to handle and look at. A story about an old fashioned car might lead you to find a toy car to show the children, or a photograph of an old fashioned car. Or if

72

the show dealt with African animals, take the children to the zoo so they can see for themselves exactly how big an elephant is. When a show is about other countries or other times, you might be able to find a book in the library that will give the children another experience with the concepts introduced.

Often there will be shows on television portraying some classic, such as *Lassie* or *Black Beauty.* Get the book from the library that these shows were adapted from. Read parts of these to the children and compare how the show was just like the book and how they were different. Which version do you like the best?

analyze the things the children see

Do you believe every thing you see and hear? Do the children? You can help the children become thinkers as they watch TV. Does the candy really melt in your mouth and not in your hand as the man said on TV? Let's try it and see. Send in for the toy advertised on the box of cereal. Does it run as fast as it did on the TV commercial? Is it as large as it appeared on TV?

Continue to ask children to form their own opinions. When they say they like a particular commercial or show, ask them why. When they answer, "It was good," dig a little deeper. "What part was good?", "Why was it good?", leading them to analytical thinking.

demonstrate your attitudes

Keep showing the children that they can trust you and respect you and that they are safe and secure in your care. Show them, even though they see people hitting and fighting on a television show, that it is indeed better to talk things over rather than fighting. Show them often and tell them many times, that you respect them and that you will help them to relate to others.

There will be times when you and the children will enjoy and benefit from a carefully selected television show. However, it's easy to fall into the trap of using television as a babysitter, and this you should try to avoid. When there is an appropriate program, try to watch it with the children, giving them some experience to go with the show, and helping them to think about the things they have seen. **Remember** that children should not be allowed to spend all of their free time with a television set. See to it that they have time to read, to play, to run outdoors, to have a friend to play with, and to have all of the other real experiences that build strong men and women. Television has its place—but it shouldn't take first place.

Learning About Food

Sitting in his high chair, pulling and kneading a piece of bread dough, the nine-month-old watches the caregiver making bread. Perhaps this experience—or the tasting of a slice of orange or raw potato—gives the child his first opportunity to learn about food. By the next year the same baby will be able to mold his bread into a bun, or press a cookie cutter down to cut a gingerbread man, and the following year he will be able to help the caregiver mix and measure, and maybe even help her set the oven thermostat to the right temperature.

Learning to enjoy foods, and to become acquainted with a wide variety of foods is a lifetime experience. When children are allowed to help with food preparation they learn many things. While you're fixing dinner or lunch, let the children work with you.
- Take a bunch of broccoli, let the children feel it, wash it, break it into pieces.
- Taste the raw broccoli, use the words raw, crunch, flowerette and stalk.
- Cook some of it and taste it for lunch, how is the cooked different from the raw? How has it changed?

Introduce a new food at snack time. Bits of raw carrot, turnip, melon or whatever is new to the children, can be cut into small pieces and served to them for a snack. If the food is new to both the child and his family, he can take some of it home with him.

cooking

Cracking an egg, watching the liquid slide into the dish, seeing it change as it cooks, is a valuable experience for children. When children can help you cook they feel very grown-up, and they learn. Remember both boys and girls enjoy and benefit from cooking experiences.

As children cook with you they learn:

- that the printed word has meaning as you read a recipe to them.
- to work together to make jello or pudding.
- how to use a measuring cup and to count how many tablespoons.
- the meaning of words like dissolve, melt, jell and boil, slippery, scramble, poach, whip, fold, blend, and steaming.

Even the very simplest cooking experiences is challenging and interesting to the children. A child may be able to begin by making his own peanut butter and jelly sandwich, or by stuffing as much cream cheese into a celery stick as he can. Spearing pineapple chunks and cheese cubes on a toothpick to make a 'kabob' is a real accomplishment.

As soon as the children become comfortable with simple food preparations, familiar with the utensils and able to handle the routines of hand washing and safety measures, you can let them do more complex cooking.

The boys and girls can make instant pudding. The measuring of the milk, and the stirring are exciting experiences for the child. You can add variety to the pudding by adding:
- a crushed up peppermint stick
- chocolate chips
- toasted coconut
- left over fruit

Let the children help you prepare vegetables. A potato peeler lets the children try their hand at peeling a potato or carrot. They can really enjoy the experience of breaking the ends off of string beans.

Or make applesauce with them. Each child can peel an apple with a potato peeler, and can cut it to remove the core and seeds in order to place it in a pan. When you have a pan of apples, add a little drop of water, just to begin the cooking, some sugar, and if you like, cinnamon. Let the children taste the applesauce before you add the sugar. How does it taste? Now add the sugar, cook it a little longer and taste again. What is different this time? What did you like the best?

Baking activities are easily managed by the children and thoroughly enjoyed as a special activity on a rainy day when they can't go out to play. If you are nervous about baking with children begin with a prepared mix. You can purchase small inexpensive box mixes just the right size to fit into a child-sized dish. The children can measure the water, break the egg and stir the mix themselves. Set the thermostat of the oven, and help them to watch the numbers on the clock so they will know when their cake, cupcakes or cookies are finished.

Make bread. The yeast smelling so richly, growing, and changing is a real experience itself. The dough can be pulled, punched, kneaded, and rolled. And the smell of baking is unforgettable. School age children especially enjoy the experience of baking bread.

Children learn about foods by actually experiencing them. However, there are other activities that can help. Take a trip to the store to see how many different types of fruits are available. Or go to the store to buy things you'll need to make vegetable soup—let each child pick a vegetable they want in the soup. Take the food home, wash it, cut it, and make a nutritious soup for lunch.

When you read a story to the children, you will find food mentioned often. When you tell the children the story of the Three Bears, fix them some 'porridge' (oatmeal), for a snack, and when you talk about Little Miss Muffett, eating her 'curds and whey' let them taste some curds and whey (farmer's or cottage cheese). Taste blueberries when you read *Blueberries for Sal,* and try a piece of maple sugar candy after reading the story of the *Biggest Bear.*

All of these experiences will help children to develop good attitudes about food they eat, teaching them to enjoy a wide variety of foods, and the knowledge that food builds strong bodies and minds. You can use your own imagination to think of the many things children can learn and enjoy in the kitchen.

Indoor Games for Something Different

Feel It—Take a box, seal the lid on it, and cut a hole, just big enough for one hand on the side. Inside the box put something round, smooth, soft, rough, prickly, sticky, square. Ask the children to put their hand in the box and find the thing that is smooth, or rough. You might also use little plastic toys of people, animals, and cars, and have the children feel for the cow, the man or the truck.

Button, Button, Who Has the Button?—Children sit together in a circle, the child who is 'it', leaves the room. Give some object, a button, spool, or marble to one child to hold in his hand. Ask all of the children to pretend they are holding the button.

'It' comes back in the room and tries to find who has the button. The closer he comes to the button, the children say warm, warmer, and the farther away he goes, they say cold, colder. When the button is found the child who has it is 'it'.

Guess What I'm Doing—Everyone will take a turn to pretend to be doing something, like ironing, washing their face, climbing a tree, without saying anything. The person who would be pretending to iron would move his arm back and forth.

The other children try to gues what the child is doing. When someone guesses correctly, he gets to be it. (Help the younger children by giving them an idea whispered in their ear.)

Surprise Bag—Put something in a brown paper bag. Seal it. You might put a new piece of food, an onion, melon, apple, in the bag, or some new toy, a book, ball or truck. Ask the children to feel the bag and see if they can guess what the surprise is. After everyone has had a turn, open the bag and eat or play with the surprise.

Animal Sounds—Mount a number of pictures of different animals on cardboard cards. One picture to a card. Put these face down on the floor and ask the child to pick one up and look at it without showing it to the other children. He will then make the sound of the animal pictured mooing like a cow, or mewing if the picture is a kitten. The other children will try to guess the animal picture he saw.

Indoor Sand Play

Playing in the sand is one of the favorite pastimes of children of all ages. They pour the sand back and forth, watching it pile up, or they build cities, roads and castles with damp sand. You can give children the opportunity to play with sand, or a similar material inside your house.

In a small plastic dishpan, or baby plastic bathtub, put about an inch or two of any type of dry material that will pour. You might try:

- dry beans
- dry cornmeal
- used, dried coffee grounds
- salt
- uncooked, dry rice
- sawdust shavings

Add some plastic containers, measuring spoons, cups, plastic bottles, boxes with lids, and small pots and pans. The children will measure and pour, pile the materials, and use it just as they would sand or dirt out-of-doors. If you are concerned with mess, cover the area with newspapers, and teach the children to sweep up any stray material.

Be certain that the younger children are not able to put the beans in their ears or noses, and that the children are beyond the age of mouthing things to find out more about them.

When children get tired of the indoor sand play, bring out the bathroom scale. Ask them to find out which container weighs the most—when filled with beans—the red cup or the blue cup? Or they can find out how many cups of rice it will take to fill the red bucket. You might ask the children which container is the heaviest when filled, or which is the lightest. Children of many ages will find this indoor experience with dry material fun, fascinating and educational.

Indoor Water Play

Children of all ages are fascinated with water. The baby splashes in his bath, the toddler will wash his hands over and over just to have the pleasure of playing in water, the preschooler finds it fascinating to see what happens when he pours water into a sieve, and the school age child still enjoys the relaxing, soothing experience of splashing in water.

Take advantage of the children's natural love and interest in water, and they will be busy and occupied for hours.

Water play is most convenient outdoors, on a warm, sunny day, with the children in bathing suits or old clothes. However, you can make some arrangements for indoor water play.

- Children may be able to stand at your sink and safely play in the water.
- You might, on some days, draw a shallow bath, and let the children splash in the tub, taking a bath at the same time. Be sure to watch them closely, however.
- You can put some water in a shallow plastic dishpan or old baby's plastic bathtub. Put the dishpan on the floor that has been covered with a plastic sheet or newspapers. Or you could put the dishpan on a chair, again covering the surrounding area with newspapers.
- Cover the children with aprons cut from a plastic shower curtain, or with a cut down man's shirt, if you feel it necessary.
- Add plastic containers, spoons, cups, old detergent bottles and watch the children enjoy their play.
- You can keep things under control, stopping children if they get out of hand, and keeping a towel, sponge, and small mop handy for them to help with their spills.

When children seem tired of pouring the water back and forth, you can increase their interest by:

- Adding a squirt of liquid soap (not detergent which may burn their hands). With the soapy water the children can wash dishes, or clothes. Someday you might give them paper straws to blow into the soapy water and let them enjoy the bubbles.
- Adding a few drops of food coloring to the water. This will help the children to see that water takes on the shape of its container and, with plenty of clear plastic containers, adds interest.
- Gathering up a variety of household things —a wooden spoon, plastic cups, a stone, a ball of aluminum foil, a fork—and have the children find out what will sink and what will float.
- Giving them different things to play with— a laundry sprinkler is good for squeezing and squirting, a piece of rubber hose, a funnel, a piece of floating soap, a sieve, muffin tins, and measuring cups and spoons.

Listen to the children as they play with water.

- What words are they using? Can you give them new words? Full, damp, sudsy, not enough, more than?
- Are they counting? Can you ask them how many red cups of water fit into the large plastic container?
- Are they finding out what happens to the newspaper when it gets wet, or where the water goes in the sponge?

Water play is fun any day of the year for children of all ages. It is especially useful on a rainy day, or a day when tempers are short and frustrations are piling up. You'll be amazed at how quickly a dishpan of water for the children to play in calms tempers, relaxes tensions, and relieves frustrations.

OUTDOOR PLAY ACTIVITIES

You don't have to live in the country to let children play outdoors. A yard is wonderful to play in, but children in a city apartment house, or other place without a backyard, still enjoy outdoor play.

There are very few days when you *are not* able to go outside. Even on a rainy day—a soft, warm rainy day—you can put on boots, rain coats, take an umbrella and enjoy a walk in the rain. Children, protected from the weather, learn about their world as they explore every puddle on the sidewalk, and poke into the wet mud. During the cold days of winter it's fun to walk in the crisp snow, or try to slide on a patch of ice. The windy days of spring find you outdoors with the children flying kites, blowing bubbles or sailing paper airplanes, and those long hot days of summer are just right for running through a sprinkler.

If you do not have a backyard, you should be able to find some place near your home to take the children for outdoor play.

Sometimes a church parking lot, school playground, YMCA yard, or a city park or playground, may be in walking distance. If these things are not near you, you can still take the children outdoors for some of the activities described in this manual.

Creative Play

Any art activity the children have done inside can be taken outside.

- give the children a coffee can filled with water and an old paint brush—they will paint the town
- take some paints outside and paint large cardboard boxes
- chalk is fun outdoors and the children can draw large pictures on the concrete sidewalk. The next rain washes the area clean again. You can get large chunk chalk from the paint store.
- take some broken crayons outside and some thin paper. Show the children how to make 'rub' overs. Lay the paper over some surface, and crayon down. Watch the texture appear.
- on another day take some paper plates and some strong glue outside. Let the children gather dry seeds, leaves, stones or twigs and paste these on their plates in a collage.

Science

Use the children's outdoor play time to acquaint them with the world around them.

- plant some seeds or bulbs around your house, and watch them grow.
- notice how the growing things in your neighborhood change with the seasons
- observe all the living things you find outside. Even in the middle of a busy city you can see insects at work. Follow the path of the ants. Where are they going? What are they doing?
- watch a beetle
- find a worm, where does he live?
- catch a snail

You don't have to live in the country to give your children some clear plastic sandwich bags, on a windy day, to see if they can catch a bag of wind. Can you see the wind inside your bag? Can you feel it? What will happen if you poke a tiny hold in your bag? Buy a kite and

fly it, or play with a pinwheel.

Wash something outside. Why is it drying in the sun but not in the shade? Make soap bubbles with dishwashing liquid. What's inside the bubbles? Why are the bubbles different colors? Give each child a paper cup with a little soapy water in it and a straw to blow in. Tell the children to blow into the straw, not to suck the soapy water. They will be delighted with the myrids of soap bubbles blowing in front of them. Why does the bubble pop?

Play with shadows. Play shadow tag. The person who is it tries to tag another person by stepping on his shadow. Take a piece of chalk and draw around your shadow. Don't be afraid if you don't know all about shadows, or wind and bubbles. You don't need to know all of the answers, you only need to be able to wonder with the children over our physical world.

Manipulative Play

Plastic containers and old plastic cups can be used outdoors for the children to collect and sort things they find outdoors. They may gather all of the small stones they find, the acorns or sticks. You can help the children count these collections, or just let them play with them in their own way.

If you have a yard some part of it could be reserved for children's digging. Digging in the dirt or sand gives children a variety of experiences, and it gives them a measure of control and understanding over their world. Don't be too worried about the children getting dirty; you can wash them off before they go in, or, on a hot summer day, they can run through a sprinkler before going back inside.

Ask a builder to give you some sand or gravel for your yard. Do you remember that wonderful 'sand between the toes' feeling? Add some sifters, sieves, colanders, pots and other containers of various sizes and shapes for the children to play with in the sand. Let the children use water with the sand. It's impossible to build with dry sand. Give them a bucket of water, squirt detergent bottles of water, or fix a hose to reach the sandbox.

Physical Play

It's good to play outside or to catch your shadow, but the purpose of playing outdoors should be to exercise growing bodies. You should try very hard to give the children some place to run, jump, hop, climb or roll, and to provide some equipment that encourages these activities.

Swing sets and metal slides are very expensive, as well as dangerous. You must always supervise children; especially the younger ones, very carefully with swing sets, for they may walk in front of a swing.

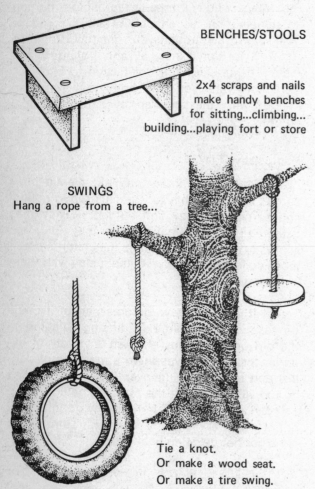

BENCHES/STOOLS

2x4 scraps and nails make handy benches for sitting...climbing... building...playing fort or store

SWINGS
Hang a rope from a tree...

Tie a knot.
Or make a wood seat.
Or make a tire swing.

Rather than purchasing a swing set for the children, you might have a large tree, a metal or wood frame that you could attach a rope to. You can make a huge knot in the end of the rope for a 'seat', or you can tie a tire to the end of it. These swings are more fun, and give the child's imagination something to work on.

Some family day care homes have built equipment for the children to climb on.
- Old tires from the gas station, planted in upright positions, give the children something to climb or jump off.
- A large tree trunk hauled into the yard is an interesting climbing structure.
- Old tires, placed in a row, can be used by children to jump in, out of, and over. They can be pushed, rolled or stacked.
- Any old log, several logs laid end to end, a board placed on its side, or even bricks partially buried in the ground, encourage the children to try their hand at "tightrope" walking, and form a balance beam.
- Boxes and boards give physical exercise for children out-of-doors. Any type of box, cardboard cartons, packing crates, soft drink containers, cantaloupe boxes, can be used. Go to the nearest market and see what they will give you.
- A wide assortment of balls of various sizes and weights is good to have. The youngest children enjoy the simple experience of dropping a small ball over and over, and laughing at you as you run to get it and return it to them. Around the age of two, children like to catch a ball while seated on the ground with their legs spread apart. The preschool children will practice bouncing, catching and throwing a ball, and school age children can play organized games.
- Wheel toys are expensive. You might, however, find well repaired beautifully painted and running wheel toys at the nearest Goodwill for very little money. A wagon and a wheelbarrow are often more practical wheel toys for the children.

Outdoor play does not mean that you will be free to go inside and do your work. Outdoor play may be free for the children, but your job has taken on new responsibilities. You must watch the children carefully to see that they are in no danger of getting hurt as they run and play. You must also be there to help them learn.

Talk to the children as they play, use concept words as the children climb in and out of boxes. Ask them to go IN a box, or say to them, as they climb, "Now you are OUT of the box." When they climb ON something, "Now you are

ON the TOP of the box" or you are *under, behind, beside,* or *next* to something.

Swing them on the tire swing, chanting UP and DOWN, UP and DOWN, Margaret likes to swing UP and DOWN. Ask the children what is *heavy,* what is *light,* tell them the names of *wet, cold, dry, sticky, rough* and *prickly* things outside. If you have to walk to the playground, or just walk around the neighborhood, tell them the names of the things you see . . . this is an evergreen tree, this is a cricket, this is a maple tree.

Children can learn many things playing outdoors. When the children have many things to explore, and different materials to experience, they are learning. With boxes, boards, sand, water, shovels and tires, the children will have the opportunity to use all of their muscles and imaginaton as they push, pull, lift, and haul, create forts, houses, pirate ships and secret hideouts.

Taking a Walk

Everyone enjoys the excitement of doing something new and different. The children in your care—whether infants, preschoolers or preteens—will enjoy and benefit from seeing new places and people.

A walk around the block, a visit somewhere, or just going outside can mean a chance to see more of the world.

When you take a walk with children they:
- learn about their community
- acquire new words as they talk about the things around them
- have a common experience to play out when they return to the home
- learn how to observe their environment more closely
- enjoy a change from the usual routines

Your first walk may be taken right inside your home. There is much to see, wonder about, talk about and learn about in your own house or apartment. Where is the furnace? Let's follow the pipes and see where they go. What happens to the water when it goes down the drain . . . follow those pipes. What is a fuse box? Where is it?

Take a trip in your home to see how many different materials were used to make it. Can you find any name for the children—plaster, metal, wood, bricks, tiles, ceramic and paper? Take a trip to see how many different sounds your feet can make . . . do they tap on the kitchen floor, slide softly on the carpet, and clunk on the concrete of the basement floor?

How many different machines do you have in your home? Take a walk and see. What machines are in the kitchen . . . an egg beater, a toaster and stove? How about the front room? Are there any machines in the basement?

What colors can you find in your house? How many red things do you see in the front room, the kitchen, the hallway? How many round things can you find right inside your house? Why not take a trip and see?

An apartment building is a wonderful place for a trip, there are so many things to see. You can ride all the way up and down on the elevator, visit the manager's office, the superintendent's work room, and the basement laundry or storage rooms.

A walk through your home could be taken when the children first come to you. After they are familiar with their surroundings, you can take them on a trip outside of your house. At first you can stay in your yard, or around your building. Look at your house from the outside. If you live in an apartment building can you find the windows that are yours? Which window is the bedroom? The front room?

What materials were used to make the building? Bricks, cement, glass? How many things can you feel on the outside of your house? Is the metal railing smooth? Are the bricks rough? How do you think the wood feels? What shapes do you see on the outside? Is there anything that's square, round or triangular? Count the windows.

From your own yard, look up into the sky. How many things do you see in the sky . . . telephone wires, antennas, airplanes, clouds? How do things look when you look up at them?

Now go a little farther on the walk. Take the children with you around the block. But before you do, take time to plan carefully. Be certain that the children know where they are going and why they are going. The purpose of a trip might be just to feel the wind on their backs, or to buy something at the store. You will also want to be sure that the parents have given you permission for the trip, and know where you will be with the children, even if it's just down the street.

Find out where the children have been before and what their interests are now. If all of the children have been to the corner fire station many times and show little interest in it, a trip somewhere else may be beneficial. If, however, they still show interest in the fire station, playing firemen and talking about them, another trip there may be fun.

Children do gain from going to the same places over and over again. They learn something new on each trip, and each trip could be taken with a different goal in mind. One day you might visit the store to buy things to make soup, another day to see the cash registers and scales, and still another to watch the delivery trucks being unloaded.

Before you take the children anywhere, visit the place yourself. Check for safety hazards, discuss with the person in charge, your ideas for the trip, and check about bathroom facilities.

Prepare the children for the walk. If you are planning to go to the library tomorrow, talk it over with them the day before. Let the children decide what they will do when they get to the library. What do they want to see? Will they be going to get a library card? To hear a story? To find a special book?

When you are thinking of going somewhere unfamiliar to the children, perhaps to the neighborhood TV repair shop, tell them something about what they will see. You might tell them why television sets need repairing, and what things the man uses to fix them. Show them pictures or read stories to them that describe the place they will go to. Ask the children to tell you what they want to find out or ask the man when they get there.

As you walk with the children you will want to follow safety measures. The younger children may ride in a stroller, with each of your preschoolers holding another's hand. You might sing a song as you walk, or chant . . . "We're going to see the bakery, the bakery, the bakery."

Teach the children to understand and follow traffic and safety signs. Point them out to the children, and explain why you are stopping to look before you cross the street at the yield sign, and why you have stopped to wait for the traffic light to turn green before you cross. If you take the children a little further than usual, or if there are unusual hazards along the way, ask a friend, neighbor to come with you.

Children can indeed walk farther than imagined. Do schedule your trip when the children are well rested, usually in the morning, or following the afternoon nap. You will not want to walk with the children when the sun is very hot, or it's too cold or windy. If the trip is for a long distance, you might plan some rest stops. Sitting in a park, on a bench or under a tree you can give the children a piece of fruit you've brought along and prepared for them, or a drink of water from a thermos.

Go for a short walk to:
- see the neighbor's flowers . . . what colors are they? What are their names? What is the neighbor's name?
- see how many signs you can find . . . are there signs on cars and trucks? What do they say? Are there signs without words? How many traffic signs do you see?
- count the number of trees on your block . . . how many have shiny leaves? What are the names of the trees?
- go to see the hole where the men are working . . . what are they doing? Can you see down inside the hole, under the street?
- watch the corner policeman at work . . . does he make any signs with his hands?
- how many homes have TV's . . . count the antennas you see.
- stand on a busy corner and see how many different kinds of shoes the people are wearing . . . how many different kinds of clothing do you see?
- wonder where the people are that came in the cars parked along side the street?
- how many houses have steps in front of

them . . . fences, grass, flowers, white plaster swans?

- watch the people get on a bus . . .where is it going?
- count the trucks you see . . . how many different kinds of trucks did you see? How many cars did you count? How many wheels do you find on things?
- go outside to watch the street cleaners, the delivery man, wait for the mailman.
- go outside to walk in the fog . . . how far can you see in the fog?
- fly a kite in the wind . . . look up at the sky and watch the clouds go by.

Nearby stores, shopping centers and market places offer endless possibilities for trips. The three year olds enjoy the 'behind the counter' trip, where they can actually go behind the counter to see what's there. The grocery store, supermarket, butcher store, gas station are continually appealing to the children.

A gas station offers a really sensory experience. The oil, tires, gasoline all smell so richly, and the men do so many interesting things to the cars with their machines, pumps, lifts and tools. The laundromat, the cleaners, beauty and barber shops, hamburger stands, printers, motels and other places of business are good trip possibilities.

Celebrate the first day of spring, a sunny day or an Indian summer fall day by packing a picnic lunch and going to the park. Take a bag with you to collect any treasures you might find leaves, rocks, or wild flowers. Listen for the sounds of the birds, the cars, lawn mowers, or the builders. At the park ask the children to find a leaf like the one you're holding, or to find all the yellow leaves they can, or all the smooth brown stones.

Visit all of the community services in your neighborhood.

The librarians usually can arrange to have a special storytime for you, and will welcome the children. The policemen and firemen, sanitation men, all have specially trained personnel to talk to the children.

See if, somehow, you can arrange for the children to visit their mother and father at their work. Sometimes this is very difficult to do, but it's well worth the effort to have the child see where his parents work, what they do and how they do it. A trip to their parent's place of work can strengthen family ties.

After the trip the children usually will need to rest. They might need some juice or other refreshment. Often they will need time to think about the things they saw before they can begin to talk about them. By the afternoon, or the next day, the children may draw pictures of their trip and tell you about their impressions. You may want to thank the grocer, baker, policeman, whoever you visited, with a note or picture. The children can draw a picture, telling you the story about it. You can write this story on their picture, and mail it to the person who assisted you on the trip.

Children will act out the things they saw on a trip. Provide a few play props to help them. Following a visit to a restaurant they may be helped to act out their experiences if you give them a pad of paper, a pencil, a tray and some plastic dishes. A trip to the gas station may find them playing 'gas station.' A bicycle pump and some old inner tubes would be good props for these children.

Sometimes you do not even need to leave your home to acquaint children with the social world. Take advantage of all of the people who come to your house, or who live near you to teach the children about their social world. Talk to the repairman who may visit your home, ask him to show the children his tools and if he has time explain to them what they are for. When the mailman comes to your building let the children talk to him. He can tell them how he knows where to put each letter, how he has to sort his mail before he leaves the post office.

You might have a neighbor or a friend who does something special that might be of interest to the children. Perhaps a grandmother knows how to crochet and would come to show the children how quickly she can take a piece of yarn and turn it into a flower. The nurse from the public health clinic, or a dental aide might be able to come and talk to the children about their work.

Trips lead to discussion. What will you do when you grow up? What do your mothers and fathers do now? What uniforms did we see today? What did they mean? Why do you think people wear uniforms? A trip teaches the children that around the corner, under a stone, right next door, they can find people, places or things that are new and exciting.

Most importantly of all, a trip in the community teaches the children that they are a part of their neighborhood. They begin to develop a pride in themselves and their community as they become aware of the role they have as a member of that community. They learn to value the community as they understand the services it gives to them—police, fire, water, communication and transportation. Trips in the neighborhood can help the children to begin to know and understand their community, involving them as participating members in the daily life of the wider world.

FOODS FOR CHILDREN

Infants—The First Year of Life

Feeding schedules for infants should be flexible and adapted to each infant's needs. Formula, breast milk, or milk ordinarily accounts for a major proportion of the total calories and various essential nutrients during the first months of life. The parents, with their physician, will determine the infant's food and feeding schedule. Some parents will bring the baby's formula for the day, others may give the caregiver instructions for preparing the formula.

As soon as he is able to sit without support, the baby should be placed in a high chair for part of the feeding time. The time he spends in the chair can be increased gradually. When solid foods are first introduced, it is best to put only a small amount of food on the tip of a spoon and let the infant suck it off. A little time may be necessary for him to get used to the feel and taste of it.

The solid foods you feed the baby will be determined by his parents and physician. It is usually wise to add only one new food at a time. If a child refuses a new food the first time it is offered, do not force him to eat it. Wait a while before offering it again.

During the later half of the first year, the baby may be interested in cup feeding and should be encouraged by allowing him to hold the cup with a small amount of water, milk, or juice. Weaning should follow the baby's lead. Frequency of bottle feedings may be decreased as he takes more milk from the cup.

Between seven to nine months of age, most babies are ready for foods of coarser consistency—mashed, chopped or junior foods—and after he has enough teeth, foods like toast, Zwieback and crackers can be offered. When the baby shows interest in picking up small objects, particles or crumbs and putting them in his mouth, he is ready to be offered bits of food to pick up and begin finger feeding. Chunks of cooked meat or vegetables, cubes of cheese, or wedges of fruit such as banana or peeled apple are good finger foods.*

Suggested Daily Meal Plans for Infants Six Months to One Year
Breakfast
Cereal (iron fortified)
Egg
Formula or milk
Mid-Morning
Orange juice
Noon Meal
Vegetable
Meat
Formula or milk
Mid-Afternoon
Formula or milk
Crusty enriched bread or crackers
Evening Meal
Cereal (iron fortified)
Fruit
Formula or milk

*Nutrition and Feeding of Infants and Children Under Three In Group Day Care. U.S. Department of Health, Education, and Welfare, Public Health Service, Maternal and Child Health Service, Rockville, Maryland, 1971.

Foods and Feeding from 13 Months to Three Years

During the second and third years of life, the child grows much less rapidly than during the first year.

It is important to continue providing those foods which help to meet the child's needs for growth and activity. The gradual extension of diet begun during the first year is continued throughout the preschool period.

Larger servings of meat, fish, and eggs, as well as fruits, and vegetables and milk, provide the protein, minerals and vitamins required by the preschooler. The increased energy needs of the child as he grows older are provided for by larger amounts of cereals, bread, butter or margarine, potatoes, and other foods as his appetite demands.

Children should be given small sized portions and allowed to have extra helpings if they want. A child will not eat the same amount every day. Appetites vary and food "jags" are common. If these normal variations are accepted without comment, feeding problems usually do not develop. Serve the foods the child's family does.

Suggested Daily Meal Plans for Children 13 Months to Three Years

Breakfast
Fruit or juice
Cereal (iron-fortified)
Milk

Mid-Morning
Milk or fruit or vegetable juice
Whole grain or enriched bread

Lunch
Lean meat, poultry, fish or egg or alternate
Whole grain or enriched bread
Fruit
Milk

Mid-Afternoon
Milk or fruit or vegetable juice
Enriched crackers

Evening Meal
Meat, poultry, fish, egg, or alternate
Vegetable
Whole grain or enriched bread
Fortified margarine or butter
Fruit or plain pudding
Milk

A Sample Daily Food Plan for Children 13 Months to Three Years

Foods	Amount Each Day	Average Size Serving
MILK (whole, evaporated, skim, etc.) Cheddar cheese may be used occasionally in place of milk	2-3 cups	½ to 1 cup (4-8 ounces)
MEAT, POULTRY, FISH, EGGS as alternate: cooked and mashed dried beans or dried peas, cottage cheese, smooth peanut butter may be used occasionally	1-2 servings	2-4 tablespoons
VEGETABLES—FRUITS A dark green or deep yellow vegetable for vitamin A. Fruit or vegetable high in vitamin C. Other fruits and vegetables including potato	4 or more servings	
BREADS AND CEREALS Whole grain or enriched. (Choose a cereal fortified with iron for the child 18 months and under)	4 or more servings	¼ cup cereal or ½-1 slice bread

VITAMIN D—Present in vitamin D-fortified milk, or may be supplied as a concentrate if prescribed by a physician.

PLUS OTHER FOODS
Other foods such as margarine, butter, or other fats and simple desserts such as milk puddings and fruit desserts, may be used to satisfy the child's appetite and to provide energy.

Foods and Feeding for Preschool Children

Children's appetites, like adults', vary from meal to meal. One day the preschool child may polish off a large plateful, and the next day seem bored with the whole idea of food. Don't expect him to eat every meal with the same enthusiasm.

Small children may go through periods of wanting to eat the same food over and over, and then quite suddenly will refuse to eat that particular food. Requiring that a specified food or amount of food be eaten may cause eating problems.

Introduce new foods gradually. Give children the opportunity to eat a variety of foods. Make eating as easy as possible. Serve the food in a form that is easy for the young child to manage. Bite-sized pieces and finger foods are suitable for small hands. Meat cut in bite-sized chunks, vegetables cut in strips, and sections of fruit are easy for children to handle.*

*Hille, Helen M., *Food for Groups of Young Children Cared for During the Day*, U.S. Department of Health, Education and Welfare, Children's Bureau, Washington, D.C., 1960. (Out of Print)

size of servings

Children of this age manage best with small helpings, for example:

½ cup to 1 cup of milk
½ to 1 ounce of meat
1 to 2 tablespoons each of vegetable and/or fruit
½ to 1 slice of bread

Children's appetites may vary from day to day. Second servings should be available for those who want them.

There are times when some children may not feel like eating some of the food served. It is best not to make a point of those. When they are ready, they will eat.

Suggested Daily Meal Plans for Preschool Children Age Three to Six Years

Following are some suggested meal plans and sample menus. Some children may need breakfast.

Food Plan for One Meal and One Snack

Use as a guide only. Each individual child may not eat the exact amounts listed.

Morning Snack	Amount	Sample Menu
Fruit or fruit juice	⅓-⅔ cup	Orange juice
Bread and butter	½-1 slice	Whole wheat bread and butter or margarine
Noon Meal		
Meat, poultry or fish	½-1 ounce	Ground beef pattie
Vegetables	½ tablespoon (cooked)	Spinach
	2-4 strips raw	Carrot strips
Bread	½-1 slice	Whole wheat
Butter or margarine	½-1 teaspoon	bread and butter
Fruit or pudding	¼-½ cup	Chocolate pudding
Milk	½-1 cup	Milk

Foods for the School Age Child

Attention to the nutritional status and food habits of the school age child is important. Behavior problems and learning difficulties could be related to poor food habits. Increasing growth needs may mean the child has a larger appetite. Enough protein in the diet is needed so a child can grow.

School children may begin to extend the variety of foods they like, so it is important that a challenging variety of foods be available.

Snacks

Snacks may be served several times a day, depending on the time the children are in your home, and their needs. Usually a snack at mid-morning, and one at mid-afternoon is welcome. Some children, arriving early in the day, may need a breakfast snack. Those staying until late in the afternoon may need another snack before going home.

All types of food can be served for a snack; think of all of the good things to eat that children enjoy instead of cookies, candy or cake.

You could serve the children:

raisins and nuts
carrot and celery sticks
pieces of apples
orange segments
popcorn
dry cereal
tomato wedges
strawberries
banana wedges
cucumber sticks or slices
crackers and peanut butter

cabbage leaves
radishes
peaches
turnip sticks
green pepper strips
melon balls
pineapple cubes
grapes
tangerines
peas in a pod

Some Sample Menus for Noon Meals for School Age Children

Grilled weiners on bun
Potato chips
Sliced tomato and lettuce salad
Apple wedges
Milk

Cream of tomato soup
Deviled eggs
Finger sandwich with American cheese
Carrot curls
Celery stuffed with peanut butter
Peach
Milk

Baked fish sticks
Buttered potatoes
Cooked greens
Raisin oatmeal muffin, margarine, butter
Watermelon cubes
Milk

Baked chicken
Rice
Buttered green beans
Cucumber sticks
Corn bread, margarine or butter
Cantaloupe crescents
Milk

Vegetable soup
Egg salad sandwich
Green pepper strips
Fruit—jello
Milk

Spanish rice and ground beef
Buttered green cabbage
Sliced beets
Hot biscuits, margarine or butter
Milk

Sloppy Joes on bun
Buttered carrot sticks
Fresh plums
Peanut butter cookies
Milk

chapter 4

Resources for Caregivers in the Family Day Care Home

COMMUNITY RESOURCES

There are a surprising number of organizations, agencies, and associations which can be directly or indirectly helpful to you in planning your day care program. Even if you have no special difficulties, you may want to try some new activities occasionally and many community resources can help you do this.

Despite the fact that many of the groups listed below are national in scope, or part of a Federal or state government, it shouldn't be hard to find their counterparts on the local level. Often a national organization will have a local chapter (e.g., the Red Cross). A governmental program is sure to have an office connected with the city, county, or regional government. If they don't, then a quick postcard to the national organization asking for specific information will usually get you the information you want. It may be helpful to keep a supply of stamped postcards on hand so you can write immediately and not wait to find paper, pencil, and stamps.

It sometimes takes a little skill at "walking through the yellow pages" to find just how an organization is listed. If it isn't found first hand, it is probably part of a larger group (e.g., various homemakers services are often part of a larger social services agency).

Many Chamber of Commerce or similar groups publish pamphlets of civic and social organizations, complete with names of people to contact and telephone numbers. In some counties and states, the department of welfare or social services provides this information in booklet form.

Hospitals often handle referrals to clinics and a variety of supportive medical services. Schools, recreation departments, and others can also be helpful. Remember that different groups keep different hours—don't try to call your local school late in the afternoon.

Knowing what agency can handle your particular problem or need is more than half the battle. Often, jotting down your concerns and sorting through potential resources will help to zero in on the group or resource most likely to be helpful. Don't worry if your first call gets you nothing more than a polite referral. Quite often it takes three or four such referrals to locate just the information you need.

In unity there is strength. If you feel your problem is one faced by other caregivers, work together to find a solution. Agencies tend to be much more responsive to groups than to individuals. If you don't know any other day care homes, check with the local agency which licenses day care homes; they may be able to put you in touch with some.

In many communities one of the most helpful organizations in the field of day care is the local Community Coordinated Child Care Council (4-C Council). If you are unable to locate the 4-C groups in your area, you can check the local social service department or the local community action agency. They may be able to help. The 4-C groups are local committees made up of citizens, agency persons, local government representatives, charitable groups, and parents of children in need of child care services. Their goal is to provide more services for children through better coordination and understanding of persons concerned and involved in children's services. They often have a list of all the services for children and can assist you in making contact with the appropriate persons for your needs. In some communities, the 4-C Council itself assists family day care homes through a variety of services ranging from transportation тor special trips to referring parents to you.

Another group which can be of help is the local Child Advocacy program. These groups are just beginning to be set up in many communities through the auspices of the Joint Commission on Mental Health of Children. They are concerned with the planning and coordination of services to children and youth and their family. Other established community organizations, such as the Community Planning Council, Governor's Committees for Children and Youth, may also be useful.

Some of the other agencies in the community that you may be contacting or using for help may include:

Library

The librarian can help you to select books, schedule a story or puppet hour for children in the neighborhood, and aid the school age child in finding reference materials.

Schools, Day Care Centers, Head Start Programs

Contact the schools in your neighborhood. What services do they have that you could use for the children? Is there an afternoon craft hour? Could your children attend a special program at the Head Start Center?

Community Services—Police, Fire, Health

Visit these agencies to find out what services they can give to you, the children and their parents.

High Schools, Community Colleges, Universities

Find out what training is available from these institutions that you might use. They may have programs in child care, home and family life, early childhood education, and may allow their students to volunteer time in your home in exchange for learning about young children.

Other Community Services

You may be able to find volunteer services and other resources for your program by calling the YMCA, YWCA, Senior Citizens, Girl Scouts, Neighborhood Youth Program, the health clinic or the hospital.

Your family day care program is just one of the many social institutions that affect the lives of children and families in your community. Churches, schools, community action agencies, hospitals, health clinics, social services, recreation programs, all influence the quality of life in the community. You, as a family day care parent, committed to improving the lives of children, may want to become involved with other institutions in the community.

FREE AND INEXPENSIVE RESOURCES

Explore the free and inexpensive things your community can give to you that can be used by the children instead of purchased supplies. Often it's well worth your time to contact your local resources for free materials. You won't be successful in every case, but it's worth trying. If they say YES, you're ahead, and the worst that can happen is that they'll say NO.

Try

Newspapers—local newspapers may be able to give you "endrolls"—the ends from their printing—these contain enough newsprint for the children to use for an entire year.

Printers—take a large cardboard box with your name and phone number on it to your local printer. Ask him to fill the box with the scraps he would ordinarily be throwing out. Ask him to please call the number on it when the box is filled, and you can pick it up. This paper will be all sizes, shapes, textures, and colors.

Computer Centers at Universities or Other Places—they will save scrap computer paper for you, and also data cards for the children to draw on.

Grocery Stores—grocery stores, packing companies, liquor stores, shoe stores and drug stores will give you all sizes and types of boxes and containers.

Lumber Yards—even hardware stores, or cabinet makers, will give you scraps of wood for the children to build with or use as blocks.

Medical Suppliers, Clinics, Drug Stores—give tongue depressors, and that wonderful styrofoam used in packing to make collages with, to string as a necklace, or just to play with.

Thrift Shops—don't forget to shop at the local thrift shop for children's toys, furniture or other supplies.

TRAINING RESOURCES

Taking care of children is one of the most important jobs you can have. And to do the best you can you should think about different ways you can improve your skills in working with and understanding children. There are a number of ways in which you can do this, and you may find that your community offers a number of opportunities for this training. Check them out before you start caring for children if possible and then continue to think about these and other ways you can learn more about caring for your day care children.

- By volunteering for local arts and crafts programs sponsored by YMCA, Head Start, or public schools you can learn skills in many different areas.
- Health, accident and safety training is usually available through the local Red Cross or city or county health department.
- Advice on food, nutrition and meal planning may be obtained through the local health department or the Extension Service of the U.S. Department of Agriculture or a nearby University.
- Local mother's clubs, childbirth education groups, Red Cross, private doctors and clinics often offer a variety of services and training in the care of infants and young children. These may be free or quite inexpensive.
- Local community colleges, high school adult education programs, vocational education programs and universities offer excellent training for people who take care of children.
- Your University Extension Services may offer correspondence courses in child care.

Additional resources which you may find helpful are listed Section III, Chapter II, Resources for Agencies.

A GUIDE FOR BUYING TOYS

Children most often enjoy the natural materials in your home as their toys—they like to cook with you, to play in the sand and dirt, to build with the empty boxes or to play in water. However, there may be times when you will want to purchase some toys. In deciding what toys and equipment to select you should consider the following:

Ask yourself:

Can this toy be used by many different age children? Or is it only usable and safe for use by a few children of a certain age? Blocks are an example of a toy that can be used by any age child.

Can the toy be used in several different ways? Or is it a toy that has only one use? Again, a set of wooden blocks, large hollow ones or small unit blocks, can be used by the children in many different ways.

Can the toy help children to feel competent? Will it help them to develop a skill? Or will it break easily and cause them to feel unhappy? Can they do something with it? Can they make something with it? All of the creative art materials, the paints, scissors, paper, paste and crayons will allow the children to feel competent.

Can the toy be used with others? Can several children play with it? Talk about it? Use it to play together? A set of baby dolls, or a wooden play family or family of puppets would encourage the children to play together.

Can you make the toy yourself or use something in your home that will serve the same purpose? Rather than purchasing a mobile for the baby to watch make one yourself. Rather than buying blocks, save cardboard boxes for the children to build with.

Toys for Different Ages

Children of different ages need different types of toys to play with.

babies

Babies need toys that catch their eye, make soft rhythmic noises or tempt their developing muscles. If you want to purchase toys for the baby you might consider:

a string of brightly colored bells

a music box
floating bath toys
a cradle gym

older babies

An older baby has different needs, and his toys, since he will put things into his mouth and toss them to the floor, must be especially safe. Some toys you might think to buy for this baby are:

a wooden set of nesting blocks
soft balls for throwing
light plastic blocks
a set of colored stack rings
a soft washable unbreakable doll
soft toy animals
squeeze toys

toddlers

Toddlers are exploring and active, and need toys that will challenge their developing muscles and minds. If you want to purchase toys for these children you might buy:

a set of wooden 'unit' blocks (found at toy stores, or school supply)
a set of large, hollow wooden blocks
a wagon, truck or other toy to actually 'sit' in
a kiddie car
a mallet and wooden pegs set
put together wooden trains, trucks, boats
large, washable dolls

preschoolers

Preschoolers like many toys. They will continue to use the wooden blocks to good advantage, and will enjoy the riding toys. In addition you can purchase:

wooden inlay puzzles
farm and zoo animal sets
matching games
small family figures (plastic or wooden)
dolls
riding toys
creative materials—paints, crayons, paper, scissors, paste

school children

Children, 6, 7, and 8, who will be in school during the day, enjoy playing with things that give them a sense of industry, things that they can actually make something with. Buy for them:

creative materials—paints, clay, crayons, paper
view masters and slides
table games—checkers, Candy Land, monopoly, cards
complicated wooden or cardboard puzzles
weaving kits
sewing kits
wood working tools and wood

The 9, 10, and 11 year old children also need some purchased toys for their free time. If you want to buy something for these children, they enjoy:

creative materials—paints, clay, paper, chalk, etc.
sports equipment—balls, tennis equipment, ping pong sets
table games that require more skill—Clue, Life, etc.
hobby sets
basket weaving, shell jewelry kits, etc.
models to put together

BOOKS AND RESOURCES ESPECIALLY FOR MOTHERS AND CAREGIVERS

Many of these books and pamphlets are available at your local library. This can save you the expense of purchasing books on your own.

Child Development

Blossom, Marilyn, *Isn't It Wonderful How Babies Learn!*, University of Missouri—Columbia Extension Service, Columbia, Missouri 65201. This small, beautifully illustrated pamphlet gives many ideas for playing with babies.

Czuchna, Gordon, *Teach Me to Talk*, CEBCO Standard Publishing Company, 104 Fifth Avenue, New York, N.Y. 10011. Interesting, practical ways to foster children's language.

Green, C. L., Margaret, *Learning to Talk: A Parent's Guide to the First Five Years*, New York: Harper & Brothers, 1960. A very practical, yet sound book describing how children learn to talk.

Hymes, James, *The Child Under Six,*

Englewood Cliffs: New Jersey, Prentice-Hall, 1963. Discussing the child's development, this book gives an interesting account of how to foster children's growth.

Murphy, Lois and Leeper, Ethel, *Caring for Children Series,* Office of Human Development, Office of Child Development, Bureau of Child Development Services, Washington, D.C., 1970:

The Ways Children Learn
More Than a Teacher
Preparing for Change
Away from Bedlam
The Vulnerable Child

Readable, helpful booklets dealing with a variety of problems and situations faced by a family day care parent.

Shuey, Rebekah M., Woods, Elizabeth L., Young, Esther Mason, *Learning About Children,* (Third Edition) Philadelphia, Pa.: J. B. Lippincott, Co., 1969. An easy to read, illustrated basic book on child development.

Publications for Parents, Children's Bureau Publications, Department of Health, Education, and Welfare, Washington, D.C.:

Infant Care	# 8
Your Child From 1-3	#413
Your Child From 3-4	#446
Your Child From 1-6	# 30
Your Child From 6-12	#324

Guiding Behavior

The following books offer suggestions for guiding the behavior of children.

Baker, K. R., *Understanding and Guiding Young Children,* Englewood Cliffs, New Jersey: Prentice-Hall, 1967.

Becker, Wesley, *Parents are Teachers: A Child Management Program.* Champaign, Illinois: Research Press Company, 1971.

Children's Behavior, Child Welfare Division, Florida State Department of Public Welfare, 1966.

Jones, Molly Mason, *Guiding Your Child*

from Two to Five, New York: Harcourt, Brace and World, Inc., 1967.

Patterson, G., Gullion, E., *Living With Children: New Methods for Parents and Teachers,* Champaign, Illinois: Research Press Company, 1971.

Health and Nutrition

Feeding Little Folks, Chicago, Illinois: National Dairy Council, 1968. A practical handbook of sound nutrition for children.

Mississippi Head Start Training Coordinating Council, *Cooking Experiences for Young Children,* Jackson, Mississippi, 1969. A guide to cooking with young children, this booklet includes many easy to cook recipes.

Nutrition and Feeding of Infants and Children Under Three in Group Care, Rockville, Maryland, U.S. Public Health Service, Mental Health Administration—Maternal and Child Health Service, 1971. Help in menu planning, meal patterns, and nutrition for the child under three.

Creative Activities

Bits and Pieces: Imaginative Uses for Children's Learning, Bulletin #20A, Washington, D.C., Association for Childhood Education International, 1967. How to help children create with inexpensive, household materials.

Creating with Materials for Work and Play, Bulletin #5, Washington, D.C., Association for Childhood Education International, 1969. Suggestions for materials and play activities for children.

Osborn, D. Keith, and Haupt, Dorothy, *Creative Activities for Young Children,* Merrill Palmer Institute, Detroit, Michigan, 1964. Many creative activities for children are suggested.

Recipes for Fun (Activities to do at Home with Children), PAR Project, 576 Hill Terrace, Winnetka, Illinois 60093, English or Spanish, $2.00, 1971. One of several practical booklets from this organization that describes many things to do with children of all ages.

Language Activities

Arbuthnot, May Hill, *Children's Reading in the Home*, Glenview, Illinois, Scott Foresman Company, 1969. A practical guide for selecting and reading books to children.

Bibliography of Books for Children, Bulletin #37, Washington, D.C., Association for Childhood Education International. An annotated listing of books children of all ages enjoy.

Blossom, Marilyn, *Magazines and Moppets*, Columbia, Missouri: University of Missouri Extension Division, 1971. A guide to selecting magazines for children.

Pitcher, E. G., Ames, et. al., *Helping Young Children Learn*, Columbus, Ohio, Charles E. Merrill Publishing Company, 1966. Many useful activities for science, play, music, language, and others are found in this book.

Play Activities

Baker, K., *Let's Play Outdoors*, Washington, D.C., National Association for the Education of Young Children, 1966. Suggestions for playing with children outdoors.

Clare, Beth, *Why Didn't I Think of That: A Teacher's Resource Book for Early Education*, Glendale, California, Bowman Press, 1971. This book is full of attractive ideas to help keep children busy, happy and learning.

Gordon, Ira, *Baby Learning Through Baby Play*, New York: St. Martin's Press, 1970. Descriptions of play activities that help babies learn.

Gregg, Elizabeth M., (with the staff of the Boston Children's Medical Center), *What to Do When There's Nothing to Do*, New York: Dell Publishing Company, 1967. A book every parent needs to keep children busy and happy. Over 600 creative play ideas are included.

Isbell, Lou, *Toys: Tools for Growth*, Columbia, Missouri, University of Missouri Extension Service, 1971.

Play—Children's Business: A Guide to Selection of Toys and Games, Bulletin #74, Washington, D.C., Association for Childhood Education International, 1969. How to select safe, valuable toys for children of all ages.

Stein, Susan M., and Sarah T., *Three, Four, Open the Door: Creative Fun for Young Children*, Chicago, Illinois: Follett Publishing Company, 1971. Numerous activities for children.

Water, Sand and Mud as Play Materials, Washington, D.C., National Association for the Education of Young Children, 1959. Helpful hints for using sand, mud and water as children's play materials.

What is Music for Young Children?, Washington, D.C., National Association for the Education of Young Children, 1969. How to help children enjoy music.

BOOKS FOR CHILDREN

For the Very Young: 1-3 Years Old

The Real Mother Goose by Blanch Fisher Wright

This book has over 400 verses and is illustrated with big pictures, all in color, that are easy for the baby to see.

Ring o' Roses by Leslie Brooke

Lovely, colorful pictures illustrate this book which contains a few well-loved nursery rhymes.

The Big Golden Animal ABC by Garth Williams

You don't want to teach your baby the ABC's just yet, but this book, with it's amusing animals can be enjoyed.

Just Like Me by Ruth McKay

This tiny book tells the story of baby's day. The kitten drinks his milk all up "just like me."

One is One by Tash Tudor

Beautiful pictures carry a child counting through twenty.

Good Morning, Good Night by Beth Comden and Aldolph Green

This book, one of a series called Kinder Owls by Holt Rinehart and Winston, takes a child through the day.

Brown Bear, Brown Bear by Bill Martin, Jr.

Another in the series of Kinder Owls, by Holt, Rinehart and Winston. This book will delight the very young, as well as the older children.

For the Preschoolers: 3-5 Years Old

The Snowy Day, Peter's Chair, Whistle for Willie, A Letter to Amy, and *Jennie's Hat*

Books by Ezra Jack Keats are beautifully illustrated and deal in a factual manner with the exciting things that happen to young children.

Umbrella by Taro Yashima

The story of a little Japanese girl living in a big city who finds an umbrella fun.

Play with Me by Marie Hall Ets

A sensitive and charming book about a child who wanted someone to play with her.

Two Is a Team by Lorraine and Jerrold Beim

This story is about the teamwork and friendship between a black and white boy.

Everyone Has a Name by Richard Browner

Stressing the idea that everyone and everything has a different name, including races of people, fosters human relationships. Children will enjoy the illustrations and verse of the text.

Sam by Ann Herbert Scott

Sensitive story of a boy who wants to play but his family is too busy. Lovely, large illustrations and a thoughtful story.

Moy Moy by Leo Politi

Moy Moy is about an enchanting little girl from Chanking Street in Los Angeles.

Where the Wild Things Are by Maurice Sendak

A story about a boy who becomes kind of all of the wild things. Be sure your children can handle the fantasy of this story.

Angus and the Ducks by Marjorie Flack

The Angus books describe real life for the children. Simple plots, but good stories, and clear illustrations the children will enjoy. Look for other books by Marjorie Flack.

Make Way for Ducklings by Robert McCloskey

A delight for children for many years, this book with its realistic pictures humorously brings the ducklings home safely to the public gardens.

For School Age Children: 6-9 Years of Age

The Biggest Bear by Lynd Ward

The story of a boy and his pet bear that ends happily.

Did You Carry the Flag Today Charley by Rebecca Cuadill

The 7's and 8's feel very superior when they read this story of a boy who has some very funny mishaps.

Lentil by Robert McCloskey

Pure Americana and a happy ending; *Lentil* is enjoyed by children and adults alike. Also try to find other books by McCloskey for your older children, such as *Homer Price.*

Little House in the Big Woods by Laura Ingalls Wilder

No child in the United States should miss the Wilder books that carry the Ingalls family from Wisconsin westward. Children find the security of heart and emotion that weathers any storm.

Nobody Listens to Andrew by Elizabeth Guilfoile

No one listens to Andrew, they're all too busy to take the time to listen to a little boy— that is until they see that Andrew has something really important to say.

6—0 Rabbit Hill by Robert Lawson

A story about the new family that moves into the 'big house.'

Charlotte's Web by E. B. White

A story for all ages, revolving around a spider who becomes involved in some very funny happenings.

For School Age Children: 9-12 Years of Age

Golden Slippers: An Anthology of Negro Poetry by Anna Bontempo

An anthology of classics of Negro poetry for young readers.

Bronzeville Boys and Girls by Gwendolyn Brooks

Forty-one short verses on Negro history.

Bright April by Marguerite de Angeli

Bright April depicts a refreshing story of friendship between black and white children.

Roosevelt Grady by Louisa R. Shotwell

A dream of having a permanent home is close to fulfillment.

Little Navajo Bluebird by Nolan Clark

A realistic, but limited approach to the modern American Indian and his problems.

Indian Hill by Clyde R. Bulla

The story of a Navajo boy who moves from the Indian reservation to the city.

Caddie Woodlawn by Carol Ryrie Brink

A tale set in Civil War years, but more of a story of a tomboy.

Island of the Blue Dolphins by Scott O'Dell

The story of an Indian girl on an island off the coast of California.

section
III

chapter 1

A General Guide for Agencies Operating Family Day Care Programs

Because of the overwhelming need, many agencies and organizations have become involved in day care services. Welfare agencies, religious groups concerned with the well-being of children, 4-C (Community Coordinated Child Care) Councils, training specialists, industry and government agencies are engaged in efforts to provide day care. Many of these groups are concerned with setting up and operating centers for children, but some are interested in the use of family day care homes as well. These groups recognize the need for care when the mother is employed, whether it be a single parent household or when both parents are present, and for other reasons which make care in the child's own home difficult or insufficient.

While the idea of family day care is very old, the decision to become involved in its operation requires careful consideration of many factors. For example, what are the specific needs of the children? Do they need the experiences available only in a center or large group, or is a home-like atmosphere with only a few other children present the better choice? What are the functions and capabilities of the agency itself? Does it have the staff and the financial resources to carry out such a program? And what is the extent of the supportive resources in the community? Are there enough homes of high quality to provide care, and will other community resources serve these homes?

Before establishing and operating a family day care service, the agency or organization will want to examine its capabilities in terms of the functions, expertise, finances and staff required. It must also seek legal advice as to whether or not this type of service is possible under its present charter. The staff will need to locate day care homes, find the children in need of day care, offer training to the caregivers in areas of child care in which they lack sufficient experience or knowledge, and be available to supervise and guide the caregivers in planning individual and group activities in the home. The agency may need to add staff members to provide the support needed by the day care homes and the parents of the children in day care.

ESTABLISHING THE FAMILY DAY CARE SERVICE

The first task of any agency or organization interested in sponsoring a family day care home program is to assess the actual child care needs in the community it serves as well as the resources and requirements of existing public and private agencies.

Determining the Community's Child Care Needs

The people interested in sponsoring family day care will need to inform themselves about the ages and numbers of children who need care as well as their geographical distribution. Information of this kind can be found from such sources as the following:

- Head Start, existing family day care and day care centers often keep a record of families inquiring about service. The number and ages of children on the lists kept by facilities in your community will tell you at once what the immediate need is and whether or not there are children older or younger than those in the existing programs for whom no service is presently available. (Often day care and Head Start Centers do not serve children younger than 3 or 4 or older than 5. Family day care is frequently the only service which can provide for infants, toddlers and after school care where needed.)

- Local schools and well-baby clinics often have a listing of the brothers and sisters of children in the families known to them.
- The local department of social services will have records of the composition of all families receiving any form of public assistance. In addition, your local Department of Labor will have statistics on the number of working mothers in your area as well as unemployment and unemployment rates.

From such sources, you can begin to determine the nature and size of your community's need for child care service. The interested agency can move to the next task of investigating the necessary resources and requirements.

Determining the Resources Available

funding

Information on federal funds for day care programs can be obtained by contacting the regional office of the U.S. Department of Health, Education, and Welfare. A pamphlet, "Federal Funds for Day Care Projects" is a helpful guide. This pamphlet is avaliable from the U.S. Department of Labor, Women's Bureau, Washington, D.C.

Community Chests, Red Feather and other philanthropic organizations also assist day care groups with a portion of their program costs. Parents' fees can also be used to make-up a share of these costs.

neighborhood facilities

In making plans to establish the family day care service, it is important to assess the resources of the community from several points of view.

geography

Are the home of children and parents to be served within easy access of each other? If not, is transportation (suitable for children as well as parents) available, or can it be provided? How far away from home do parents work, on an average? Will it be feasible for a parent to travel to the day care home with the child and still arrive on time for work? All of these are important questions in determining where an agency should plan to locate its own headquarters as well as recruit its day care homes and may very well determine whether or not the program, once established, will be fully utilized by those who need it.

physical facilities

Since family day care is a service offered primarily in private homes, a general assessment of the condition of those homes is needed. Is an adequate number of homes available which can meet the local licensing requirements? Homes need not be either elaborately equipped or affluent. In low-income areas of marginal housing, it is often possible to find many well-maintained homes or apartments in spite of dilapidated exteriors. A little neighborhood research may uncover many suitable homes.

other services

Do not overlook the availability of related services which may prove helpful to you in your own operation. For example, child health clinics may be available for immunizations. A nearby hospital can perhaps be persuaded to take on the task of giving physical examinations to the caretakers. A neighborhood public library may be willing to set up some special story telling schedules for the children. Or, in rural areas, a bookmobile may be available to serve these homes. All such potential resources should be contacted so that cooperative arrangements can be set up as soon as your program gets underway.

Determining the Requirements to be Met

Most states have minimum requirements which must be met in order to obtain a license. Though these vary greatly from state to state, almost all cover such items as:

- maximum number of children who may be cared for in one home by the caregiver,
- health of the mother and the family in the home,
- cleanliness and maintenance of the home,
- activities to be conducted in the home,
- health of the children to be cared for.

In planning to meet your state's licensing requirements, remember that such requirements usually establish only *minimum* standards of safety for the protection of children. Conscientious agencies, therefore, will want to extend their planning beyond these legal minimums to achieve the most comprehensive and high quality service that can possibly be established with the resources available to them.

DECIDING ON COMPONENTS OF SERVICE

Besides the basic service of finding and supervising suitable homes, a sponsoring agency must decide to what extent it wishes to enlarge these basic functions. A sponsoring agency may wish to consider enrichments to the basic child-caring function such as:

Training in Early Childhood Education and in Home Economics for Caregivers

Anyone chosen to provide care for the children of others as part of a program administered by a responsible agency should have basic pre-service orientation as well as regular supervision and follow-up. An agency planning to equip adults to do a good caretaking job should explore the resources of its community to determine what kind of training is available or easily adapted to the needs of the service.

Persons caring for children in their homes may need considerable help in planning a sound program of activities as well as in budgeting their own time during the course of the day. Household chores, food preparation, outings, story time and supervised play for the children should become an established part of the daily routine of the day care home. Accordingly, any training plan must take all of these activities into account.

pre-service orientation

Many family day care agencies provide two or three days of intensive training before the day care mother is considered ready to accept children into her home. Among the topics which should be covered in pre-service training are:

- the importance of both verbal and physical communication with young children, including infants;
- techniques for handling discipline problems;
- guidance in handling childhood sexual curiosity;
- understanding sibling rivalry;
- coping with anxiety of the child at the time of separation from his mother;
- the importance of maintaining good relationships with the child's natural mother as a means of continuing the care of the child's own home into the day care home;
- an understanding of the importance of play and what children learn from it both indoors and outdoors;
- using good judgment about the choice of clothing for infants and young children in keeping with the weather;
- the importance of keeping the home safe;
- the use of money for children's food, to attain good nutrition, shopping for food and preparing it;
- identification of childhood illnesses, the circumstances under which children should be isolated, and caring for the ill child;
- the importance of maintaining sanitary housekeeping practices and good personal hygiene.

in-service training

Agencies will want to follow the orientation with a more intensive discussion of each of the foregoing subjects. This training is needed both for the sake of the educational content of the program and for the enrichment of the life of the day care parent. This second goal can be accomplished in a variety of ways. First, the agency can arrange seminars on some regular basis (possibly monthly) at which all the caregivers meet and share with each other. This can become a problem-solving session around items which they encounter in their daily work and which are of special interest to them. The seminars should be under the guidance of a skilled discussion leader who may generate intensive discussions around such topics as child development, nutrition, children's questions on sex, etc.

In order to make regular meetings possible, the sponsoring agency may find it necessary to invest some of its funds in employing part-time babysitters or home-helpers who can assume responsibility for the care of the children during the monthly hour or two that the caregiver is participating in seminars. If a play room can be staffed adjacent to the meeting room, mothers can bring the children with them.

Groups should be kept small enough that all the children can be handled. In addition, regular visits to the individual day care homes by social workers or other trained staff will do much to guarantee that a quality service combining good education, nutrition, and preventive health is given to the children. The combination of problem-solving seminars and individual home visits will also go a long way toward assuring the caregiver that she can count on the support of a concerned agency. Thus, both her interest and ability to serve would be enhanced.

further education and enrichment

As an additional step, a sponsoring agency may wish to provide basic education for the mothers caring for children in the program. As with seminar-based training, the agency may be able to draw upon the resources of a nearby college, a local high school, or other skilled individuals serving the community in a variety of ways. If the agency desires to improve the basic education of caregivers, it is best to seek a cooperative arrangement with the adult education department of nearby schools or colleges. In this way, broader education may be offered, including high school equivalency, and courses for college credit in subjects related to child development. Such a plan will serve not only to increase the skills of persons presently serving in the program but will also enable these persons to improve their economic position and perhaps move up within the agency's own structure into positions of higher responsibility.

centralized administrative and support services

In addition to the specific services listed, a sponsoring agency should consider at least some of the following services which would help to assure high quality of day care offered in the homes:

- Administrative services such as insurance and liability coverage for homes, central recordkeeping, evaluation of activities in homes, purchase of some equipment as well as central purchasing of materials, books, and supplies.
- Regular and special consultation and technical assistance to homes for routine problems as well as for special problems.
- Basic health and social services or referral of children and families to such services.
- Certain specialized services, or referral to these for children.
- Central planning and organization of field trips or special activities.
- Parent counseling for families using the day care homes.

DETERMINING COST AND FUNDING SOURCES

Once an agency has done the preliminary "homework" which has previously been discussed, in terms of (1) the number and ages of children needing care; (2) the availability and cost of an agency's headquarters; and (3) the components of service it wishes to provide, it is then prepared to draft a budget of projected expenses and potential income.

A budget for an agency serves much the same purpose as a family's budget for its household expenses. List all possible sources and exact amounts of anticipated income which, in turn, is balanced by a list of all of the expenses which the program's sponsors can reasonably expect in their first year of operation. First year budgets are invariably higher than ongoing budgets for subsequent years of operation. This happens because of the necessity of purchasing basic equipment in the initial stages. Many of these items are either non-recurring or recur so infrequently that their cost can be prorated over several years and the impact will not be felt all at once as in the first year.

Organization and Functions of Personnel

the caregivers

If an agency has determined that there are between 200 and 300 children who need care and the local licensing law permits a maximum of 6 children to each caregiver, including own children, then approximately 50 to 60 caregivers will have to be recruited. At this point, the agency will also have to decide whether or not it wants these persons to become employees of the service with regular annual rates of pay, social security, unemployment insurance and other fringe benefits, or whether it prefers to purchase their service on a stipend basis paid at a per capita rate of each child accepted into care. Both systems have advantages and disadvantages and should be considered carefully before any decision is made.

Caregivers who are salaried employees of the agency will have a greater sense of security and therefore a greater commitment to their child caring and training responsibilities. If the agency has a relationship with a group care or Head Start Center, a salaried caregiver who temporarily has no children in the home may be assigned to the center during this period as a substitute for regular staff who may be absent or as a trainee using this opportunity to enhance child care skills.

On the other hand, agencies may prefer to purchase services from the day caregivers through payment of a stipend for each child. Problems arise, however, when children are absent for reasons of illness or changes in their parents' employment, since payment to the day caregiver will cease at this point. The same is true in the event of illness of the day caregiver. This system provides considerable flexibility, but often makes for less stable service. The decision to use one or the other must be based in part on the agency's wishes and in part on its funding resources. Whatever their decision, it will enable them to arrive at a dollar figure of payment for each child served and to include this total in the annual budget.

the home-finders and supervisors

A family day care program consisting of fifty family homes serving children will need at least one and possibly two professional home-finders and supervisors. If possible, this person should have a background in social work and child welfare. Among this person's functions are:

. . . locating suitable homes

The home-finder should be well-versed in the licensing requirements in use in your state and should therefore be equipped to certify homes as licensable or not. In addition, such a person should be well-versed in the kinds of personal qualities that your agency may be seeking in persons selected to offer child care in their homes.

In addition to assessing the caregivers personal qualifications for work with children, the home-finder must also make some practical judgments about the personal qualities of other family members who will come in contact with children on a daily basis. He or she must also be able to make decisions and commit limited sums of money, where necessary, to help a prospective day caretaker equip the home adequately for a small group of children. The home-finder might have a check-list of suggested play items which he or she would be authorized to purchase for children's use in these homes.

While the home-finder will carry on the specific activities necessary for the screening and approving of homes selected for use in the program, the initial task of locating persons willing to offer their homes is one which the agency must undertake as a whole. It may be necessary to place advertisements in local papers and to post signs in such places as the neighborhood school yard, child health center, welfare center, shopping centers, laundromats, etc. A recruitment campaign should net a sizeable number of applicants who will wish to serve as family day caretakers. The home-finder can then begin the task of screening these homes for suitability.

. . . recruiting children

The same staff member who is responsible for home-finding and supervision can also serve as the intake person for the registration of children whose parents wish to use the services. The campaign to recruit children can be conducted simultaneously with the campaign to recruit homes. An office clerk can assume initial responsibility for recording such basic information as name, address, age and reasons why service is needed for families who come to register at the agency's headquarters. As soon as the home-finder has certified a few suitable homes, she should then begin the task of interviewing the parents who have registered their need for service in the agency's office. This interview will focus on the family's need for day care and any additional counseling or services which they might require. At this time also, the family can be given a list of suitable homes to consider for their children.

While some agencies reserve the right to select the home for the children, many now consider this activity the responsibility of the parents, with consultation from the agency.

. . . the caregivers

The third role to be played by the staff member responsibility for finding homes and placing children is that of supervision. This will require a regular program of visitation twice yearly at minimum, oftener when possible, to insure that the criteria initially set for approval of the home are still being maintained. This will mean also periodic re-evaluation of each caregiver's health, family situation, and continuing ability to give good care to children as well as to maintain good relationships with the parents of the children being cared for.

program aides

If an agency wishes to guarantee an educational experience to the children served in its program, it will need staff for the purpose of carrying child development techniques and skills directly into the day care homes on a regular basis. It is recommended that program aides be hired at a ratio of one to each five homes in order to permit them to give approximately one day of service per week to each home. Thus, a program encompassing fifty homes will need to employ at least ten program aides.

Program aides may be para-professionals who have been given intensive specialized training in the techniques and use of child development activities and materials. Program aides can most successfully be recruited from among persons who already show special aptitude in working with children and parents in programs such as Head Start, day care, or prekindergarten in the public schools. Program aides would be expected to visit each home at least once per week to introduce new materials and techniques for working with children.

Aides might conduct singing games and finger plays with the children on one occasion, puppetry and story telling on another, use of special art media on still another. Aides should also carry with them one or two toys or materials supplied by the agency which can be introduced into the children's experience, as well

as that of the day caretaker. On scheduled occasions the aide should be available to assume full responsibility for the children so that the caregiver can be free to attend a full-time training session.

coordinator of educational services

If the program aides are to function effectively and be equipped to present new materials and ideas to the caregivers, they will need to draw upon the special resources of a professionally trained child development person. The educational supervisor may be employed on a part-time or consultant basis as needed. An educator might be from a nearby college or university, and might be available for one or two days per month.

The educational supervisor should be available on some regular basis to conduct seminars and workshops with the program aides, to provide them with resource materials and guidance in the task of carrying out the daily responsibilities. Additionally, the educational supervisor might be called upon to conduct problem-solving sessions with the day caretakers themselves. Such sessions might include the specific learning areas involved in play activities, handling of discipline problems and maintaining effective communication with children's own parents.

the program director

Finally, any program which is to function effectively must be headed by a competent administrator who also provides a background of skills in child development or related human services.

The program director is, of course, responsible for the overall administration and supervision of all aspects of the agency's program, including the individual family day care homes which serve the children. The program director must also be the coordinator and community outreach person who establishes liaison between the day care program, the licensing or funding agency and a variety of related services throughout the community. The program director must also assume responsibility for sharing the results of these activities both with the sponsoring board and the agency's staff to assure their full knowledge and understanding of community developments and the program's cooperative role in relation to other services.

Other Budget Expenses

In addition to the cost of staff, which will be the principal expense of any day care agency, the agency will also have to allocate monies toward payment of rent on its headquarters, purchase of food to be served to children in the day care homes, purchase of office equipment for its headquarters and purchase of play equipment for use by the children in the daily program. Additionally, as indicated, there will be some occasional expense connected with meetings, and consultants called in for special purposes. A sample budget is suggested in Appendix B.

ESTABLISHING A SET OF PERSONNEL POLICIES

Maintaining good work relationships among staff, board members, and families which the program is designed to serve is the key to the effective delivery of any service to the public. Sponsoring boards must therefore make specific plans to assure that those they hire to deliver the service to the community are, in fact, doing so in the most effective manner possible.

Basic to a good working climate is a set of personnel policies which spell out exactly what you expect of staff in performance of their jobs as well as what they can expect of you. The policies should include such specifics as length of probationary period, evaluation, grievance appeal procedures, and number of paid holidays.

chapter 2

Resources for Agencies

Each of these resources, in addition to the specific services listed, may also be a resource for training groups of caregivers. Staff could be consulted about providing one or several hours of discussion for caregivers on various topics.

Special Clinics and Clinicians

Pediatric Clinics, Public Health Clinics, Maternal and Child Health Clinics, Well-Baby Clinics, Neighborhood Health Clinics, Pediatricians, Physicians, Public Health Nurses can:

- Identify, evaluate, and diagnose general health conditions of children
- Identify emotional and learning problems in children
- Refer a child with a special problem to a specialist
- Provide instruction and counseling for parents
- Consult with you on health problems of particular children or activities to promote general health of all children
- Serve as a training source for day care mothers

Mental Health Center, Child Guidance Clinics can:

- Identify, evaluate and diagnose emotional problems in children
- Identify, evaluate and diagnose learning problems
- Offer therapy and medication if necessary
- Provide advice and consultation on dealing with specific problems

Community Action Agencies, Social Service Agencies, Community Welfare Councils, Welfare Offices, Neighborhood Centers can:

- Offer financial assistance to families or refer them to other sources of financial assistance
- Provide funds for day care
- Offer family counseling services
- Offer recreational programs
- Serve as a referral source for your program
- Offer homemaker services for some families in the absence of the mother

Universities and Colleges

Education Departments, Schools of Social Work, Schools of Medicine and Nursing can:

- Place students in your program to assist you and to gain experience
- Help identify and evaluate children with special problems

Public School Systems

Teachers, Students, and Social Workers can:

- Visit the homes and work with special children who might enter their classes
- Provide students to assist you several hours a week
- Provide adult classes in child care and education

Special Schools can:

- Sponsor activities to include your children who may have special needs
- Consult with you or assist you in working with a child with special needs

Civic Groups

Lions Clubs, American Legion, Rotary, Odd Fellows, Red Cross, and other civic groups can:

- Volunteer for group activities or help with a specific child
- Donate or build equipment for you
- Transport children on special occasions

- Provide glasses or other health aids for children
- Provide training in health, child care, and safety

State Departments

State Departments of Public Health, Mental Health, Social Services, Education, and Employment can:

- Provide funds for day care training or for supportive services for special children with special needs
- Offer training or consultation
- Counseling and testing for employment

Libraries

Local libraries can:

- Offer books and story hours
- Provide bookmobiles for outlying areas
- Provide talking book machines for children with special needs
- Offer children's films

Federal Programs

Head Start Centers, Elementary and Secondary Education Act, Neighborhood Youth Corps Programs (NYC), and Work Incentive Programs (WIN) can:

- Offer training and financial assistance to families
- Provide student aides or trainees to assist you several hours a week
- Sponsor joint activities to include your children

Federal and Local Housing Authority

Federal Housing Authority (FHA) or Local Authority can:

- Provide housing for families
- Provide loans to repair your home

BOOKS ESPECIALLY FOR AGENCIES

Child Growth and Development

Baldwin, A. *Theories of Child Development,* New York: John Wiley and Sons, Inc., 1968.

Hunt, J. McVicker, *Intelligence and Ex-*

perience, New York: Ronald Press, 1961.

Lichtenberg, Phillip and Delores G. Norton, *Cognitive and Mental Development in the First Five Years of Life,* Rockville, Md.: National Institute of Mental Health, #72, 9102, 1970.

Mussen, P., Conger, J., and Kagan, J., *Child Development and Personality,* New York: Harper and Row, 1969.

Russell, David H., *Children Thinking,* New York: Blaisdell Publishing Company, 1965.

Stone, L., Joseph and J. Church, *Childhood and Adolescence,* New York: Harcourt, Brace and World, 1972.

Von den Eyken, W., *The Pre-School Years,* Middlesex, England: Penguin Books, 1967.

Wann, K. D., M. S. Dorn, and Liddle, Elizabeth, *Fostering Intellectual Development in Young Children,* New York: Teachers College Press, Columbia University, 1962.

Education of Children

Brearly, Moddly, ed., *The Teaching of Young Children—Some Applications of Piaget's Theory,* New York: Schocken Books, 1970.

Denenberg, Victor H., *Education of the Infant and Young Child,* New York: Academic Press, Inc., 1970.

Dinkmeyer, Don and Driekurs, Rudolph, *Encouraging Children to Learn: The Encouragement Process,* Englewood Cliffs, N.J., Prentice Hall, Inc., 1963.

Dittmann, Laura, ed., *Early Child Care: New Perspectives,* New York: Atherton Press, 1968.

Hartup, Willard W. and Smothergill, Nancy L., *The Young Child: Review of Research,* Washington, D.C.: The National Association for the Education of Young Children, Volume I—1967, Volume II—1972.

Hess, Robert D. and Bear, Roberta, eds., *Early Education,* Chicago: Aldine Publishing

Company, 1968.

Painter, Genevieve, *Infant Education,* San Rafael, California: Dimensions Publishing Company, 1968.

Provence, Sally A., *Guide of the Care of Infants in Groups,* New York: Child Welfare League of America, Inc., 1967.

Resources for Administrative Decisions

Boguslowski, D. B., *Guide for Establishing and Operating Day Care Centers for Young Children,* New York: Child Welfare League of America, Inc., 1967.

Costain, L. B., *New Directions in the Licensing of Child Care Facilities,* Child Welfare, 49, 1970.

Fein, G. G. and Clarke-Stewart, Alison, *Day Care in Context,* New York: John Wiley and Sons, 1973.

Grotberg, Edith H., ed., *Day Care: Resources for Decisions,* Washington, D.C.: Office of Economic Opportunity, 1971.

Mayer, G., Alaine, Krim, and Pape, Catherine, *Contributions of Staff Development in Understanding the Needs of Children and Their Families,* New York: Child Study Association of America, 1963.

For Parent Involvement

Adair, T. and Eckstein, E., *Parents and the Day Care Center,* New York: Federation of Protestant Welfare Agencies, Inc.

Day Care and Child Development in Your Community, Washington, D.C.: Day Care and Child Development Council of America, Inc., 1969.

Ginott, Haim G., *Between Parent and Child,* New York: The Macmillan Company, 1965.

Rudeman, F., *Child Care and Working Mothers,* New York: Child Welfare League of America, Inc., 1969.

Activities of Children

Brandwein, P. F. and Cooper, E. K., *Concepts in Science,* New York: Harcourt, Brace and World, Inc., 1967.

Croft, D. and Hess, R., *An Activities Handbook for Teachers of Young Children,* Boston: Houghton Mifflin Comanpy, 1972.

Dawson, M. and Frieda H. Dingee, *Children Learn the Language Arts,* Minneapolis: Burgess Publishing Company, 1959.

Engel, Rose C., *Language Motivating Experiences for Young Children,* Van Nuys, California: DFA Publishers, 1968.

Gaitskell, Charles and Hurwitz, A., *Children and Their Art,* New York: Harcourt, Brace and World, 1970.

Hartley, Ruth, Frank, L., and Goldenson, R., *Understanding Children's Play,* New York: Columbia University Press, 1952.

Jefferson, B., *Teaching Art to Children,* Boston: Allyn and Bacon, 1963.

Nuffield Mathematics Project, *I Do, and I Understand,* New York: John Wiley and Sons, Inc., 1967.

Pitcher, Evelyn Goodenough, Laher, Miriam G., Feinburg, Sylvia, and Hammond, Nancy, *Helping Young Children Learn,* Columbus, Ohio: Charles E. Merrill Publishing Company, 1966.

Sharp, E., *Thinking is Child's Play,* New York: E. P. Dutton and Company, 1969.

Sheehy, E., *Children Discover Music and Dance,* New York: Henry Holt, 1959.

The following materials may be ordered from ERIC Document Reproduction Service (EDRS) in either microfilm (MF) or hardcopy (HC), except where marked microfiche only.

1. Address orders to:

EDRS
Leasco Information Products, Inc.

Post Office Drawer O
Bethesda, Maryland 20014

2. Give the title and ED number of each item ordered.

3. Price schedule:

   a. The price for each title ordered in microfiche (MF) (transparent filmcard) is $0.65. (To read MF you need a microfiche reader, available in most libraries.)

   b. The price for each title ordered in hardcopy (HC) (photocopy reproduction) is computed according to the number of pages listed with the entry.

Pages	Price
1 - 100	$3.29
101 - 200	6.58
201 - 300	9.87
301 - 400	13.16
401 - 500	16.45
Each additional 1 - 100 page increment	3.29

4. Postage is included in the above rates. There is no handling charge.

5. Payment must accompany orders under $10.00

6. Orders must be in writing.

   Collins, Alice H., and Watson, Eunice L., *The Day Care Neighbor Service: A Handbook for the Organization and Operation of a New Approach to Family Day Care,* 1969, 63 pages, ED 049 810.

Dokecki, Paul R, and Others, *The Training of Family Day-Care Workers: A Feasibility Study and Initial Pilot Efforts, Final Report,* January 1971, 37 pages, ED 053 787.

   Emlen, Arthur C., and Others, *Child Care by Kith: A Study of the Family Day Care Relationships of Working Mothers and Neighbor-hood Caregivers,* 1971, 339 pages, ED 060 955.

   Evaluating Home Day Care Mothers Work With Young Children, Seattle Community College, Washington, 1971, 10 pages, ED 055 104.

   Galambos, Eva C., *Income Tax Deductions for Family Day Care Homes,* Southeastern Day Care Bulletin No. 1, June 1971, 7 pages, ED 054 860.

   Howard, Norma K., Comp., *Day Care: An Annotated Bibliography,* June 1971, 19 pages, ED 052 823.

   Lynch, Dollie and Kinard, Claude, *Abstracts of State Day Care Licensing Requirements Part I: Family Day Care Homes and Group Day Care Homes,* 1971, 214 pages, ED 059 760.

   Prescott, Elizabeth, *Group and Family Day Care: A Comparative Assessment,* February 1972, 22 pages, ED 060 945.

   Problems on Licensing Family Day Care Homes, Southern Regional Education Board, Atlanta, Georgia, November 1971, 19 pages, ED 058 959.

The following booklets are available from the:

Day Care and Child Development
   Council of America, Inc.
1401 "K" Street, N. W.
Washington, D.C. 20005

   Sale, June S., *Open the Door—See the People: A Descriptive Report of the Second Year of a Community Family Day Care Project,* Pacific Oaks College, 1972, 247 pages, $4.00.

   Sale, June S., Torres, Yolanda Ledson, *I'm Not Just a Babysitter: A Descriptive Report of the Community Family Day Care Project,* July 1971, 217 pages.

appendices

appendix A

Sample Family Day Care Programs

Title of Program	Sponsorship	Program Description	Special Features	Further Information
1. Licensed Day Care Operators Association Berkeley-Albany Area, Inc.	Local Licensed Family Day Care Mothers	Mothers meet monthly to discuss mutual problems and ways to improve their programs. They offer courses in first aid and early childhood education, and hope to set up a Toy Lending Library. Utilize community offerings through organization.	Program started through Office of Community Child Care Workshop series, organized and later incorporated as a non-profit association. Offers wholesale buying, group insurance rates and training.	1. Mrs. Susanne Horvath 959 Ventura Avenue Albany, Ca. 94707 2. Etta Rose, President 1337 Cornell Berkeley, Ca. 94702
2. Metropolitan Community Coordinated Child Care Committee	4-C Committee	Provides variety of services to several family day care programs in the city. Services vary according to needs of the programs. They offer: nursing assistance, social workers, training in child care, homemaker services for sick children, information and referral for families seeking child care. Local department of social services contracts with 4-C for services. 4-C then contracts with local homes and centers for service.	Services to various day care programs, homemaker services, information and referral for parents seeking day care.	Ms. Jeanne Davis 1630 S. W. Morrison Portland, Or. 97201 (501) 288-5091
3. Model Cities Child Development Program Atlanta, Georgia	Atlanta Model Cities Program & Senior Citizen Services of Metropolitan Atlanta, Inc.	Currently provides full day center care for children ages 0-3½ years old. Provided before- and after-school care in "Block Mother" homes for children 12 years and under, 1969 through 1971. Provided full day care for children 0-3½ years old in Family Day Care Homes, 1969 through 1972. Food was provided and sent out to "Homes" from a central kitchen. Currently offers employment to persons over age 55 in five centers. All staff trained in child care.	Family Day Care Mothers were salaried, not paid direct fee by parents. Central food service to Family Day Care Homes and Block Mother Units. Block Mother service for school age children (up to 12 years). Employment for persons over age 55.	Model Cities Child Development Program 363 Georgia Avenue, S.E. Atlanta, Ga. 30312 (404) 524-5621
4. Women's Educational & Industrial Union Boston, Massachusetts	Private, non-profit service organization	Union selects, trains full- or part-time day care operators. Union refers children; supplies play materials, consultants, liability insurance. Cost of care paid by welfare or parent on sliding scale.	Salary, benefits for day care mothers. Student aides, liability insurance. 6 week training, college credit available.	Women's Educational and Industrial Union 264 Boylston Street Boston, Ma. 02116 (617) 536-5651

Title of Program	Sponsorship	Program Description	Special Features	Further Information
5. Division of Day Care and Child Development of the Center for Human Services (Formerly the Day Nursery Association)	Private association	The program interviews day care mothers, trains them; also interviews and places children seeking day care. Trained assistant is provided to mother by the Division. Basic toys and equipment are provided by the Division. Medical and dental checkups are provided.	Salary for day care mothers, trained assistants, counseling for families desiring day care.	Division of Day Care and Child Development Center for Human Services 2084 Cornell Road Cleveland, Ohio 44106 (216) 621-0323
6. New York City Family Day Care Program	Agency for Child Development	Family day care homes are part of a system of centers with up to 50 homes as satellites. Educational aides assist in homes. Day care mothers may move up a career ladder. Centers often plan field trips to include family day care. They also provide equipment on a rotating basis.	Center-satellite system career ladder, educational aides.	New York Family Day Care Program Agency for Child Development 349 Broadway New York, N.Y. (212) 553-6524
7. Pacific Oaks Community Family Day Care Program	Pacific Oaks College	Selected day care mothers serve as "consultants," assisting other day care mothers and staff in dealing with mutual problems. Consultants meet monthly and are paid fees for each meeting. Student Field Assistants help out in homes two mornings per week; mobile toy-loan unit provides equipment. Six Family Day Care Mothers also participate in a cooperative nursery school program where they may bring the children in their care; thus combining a group and home experience.	Mothers hired as "consultants," Mother's Club with nursery school experience, field demonstration assistants and toy-loan units.	June Sale Community Family Day Care Project/Pacific Oaks College 714 West California Pasadena, Ca. 91105 (213) 795-9161
8. Project Playpen, Inc.	Juvenile Welfare Board of Pinellas County	A pilot program of subsidized day care which allows low-income families to place their very young children in licensed neighborhood homes. Volunteers visit each day care home at least once a week to check needs and to assist in various ways. Staff recruit and train all day care mothers, provide in-service assistance and training. Day care mothers receive a temporary subsidy of 50 cents per day for any unused vacancy, and a supplement of 50 cents per day per child for food. Community organizations and citizens actively involved in raising money and providing toys.	Volunteers to assist day care mother, provide toys and equipment, vacancy subsidy, active involvement of community.	Project Playpen, Inc. Juvenile Welfare Board of Pinellas County 3455 First Ave. South St. Petersburg, Fla. 33711 (813) 898-4161 ex. 382

appendix B

Forms for Family Day Care

Sample Family Day Care Home Emergency Plan

     In keeping with the Family Day Care Licensing Act and the requirements of the Licensing Rules and Regulations, this emergency plan is being submitted as a part of my application:

1. Physician who has agreed to be on call:

_____, M.D.
Name

_____
Address

_____
Telephone

Distance from my home: _____

2. Nearest Hospital:

_____
Name

_____
Address

_____
Telephone

3. Nearest Ambulance Service:
   Name: _____
   Address: _____
   Telephone: _____

4. Nearest Fire Department:
   Name: _____
   Address: _____
   Telephone: _____

5. Nearest Police Station:
   Name: _____
   Address: _____
   Telephone: _____

6. Nearby adult substitute on call in event of applicant's absence because of an emergency:
   Name: _____ Birth Date: _____
   Address: _____
   Telephone: _____

_____
Signature

HOME STUDY

A Home Study should be done by the licensing person in order to make the evaluation of the family and home. A suggested outline follows:

I. Family Composition

A listing of the members of the household including birthdate and age.

II. Contacts

Home visits
Office visits
Phone
Date and person(s) seen
Date and person(s) seen
Date and person or agency contacted

III. House and Neighborhood

A. Location of home, description of the neighborhood, public transportation accessible, libraries, parks, playgrounds, schools, etc.

B. Description of building, apartment—number of rooms, walk-up or elevator, housekeeping standards, available beds for naps, furnishings, play area, phone, educational materials, such as toys, books, etc.

IV. Family Members

A physical description, personality, general appearance, bearing and attitudes observed for each member of the family. Include the background of the mother and father, birthplace, length of time in city, language spoken, employment history, educational background.

V. Family Relationships

The relationship between father, mother and children. Relationship with family members not living in the home. Social and civic activities of the family. Relationship with relatives, neighbors and friends.

VI. Family Routine

Daily routines of family members, who are in the home during the day.

VII. Child Care Practices

Previous child care experiences with own and other children. Methods of discipline, toilet training. Willingness to care for children with special problems.

VIII. Health

A. Current health situation of all family members including past illnesses and operations. Regarding children: discussion of childhood illnesses and immunizations.

B. Physical examinations for every family member with X-rays and serology for eveyone over 15 years of age.

C. Follow-up with Director of special medical problems, e.g., diabetes, heart condition, obesity.

IX. Financial Management

Source of income and family management.

X. References

Three references, including a summary of the contact, name, address, phone number and relationship to family.

XI. Evaluation and Recommendation

A. DISCUSSION OF THE PROGRAM—Understanding the responsibilities of day care mother, fee schedules, willingness to participate in agency sponsored activities, training, supervision, trips, feeding. Ability to work with child's parents. Willingness to accept children without regard to race or religion. Any religious restriction on activities.

B. SUMMARY—
The strengths and weaknesses of the family, worker's impressions, recommendations as to number of children and ages to be placed. Any special suggestions for supervision.

ASSOCIATION

Parent's Agreement:

I consent to the enrollment of my child/ren_____
with the _____ Association and agree that the _____
Association shall not be responsible in case of sickness or injury of this child/ren while in the
attendance of an Association facility or in transit to and from the facility.

I give my consent for my child/ren to take part in field trips or excursions under proper
supervision.

I agree to pay the weekly fee in advance and I will carry out the rules and regulations of the
Association.

I further agree that in case of accident or injury, emergency medical care may be given in the
event that I cannot be contacted immediately.

_____
Mother's Signature

_____
Father's Signature

_____
Witness

_____
Date

This form would be kept by the family day care mother and filled out daily

DAY CARE CHILD ATTENDANCE RECORD

Name of Child _____   Category _____

	1	2	3	4	5	6	7	8	9	10	11	12	13	14	15	16	17	18	19	20	21	22	23	24	25	26	27	28	29	30	31	Total	Absent	Present
JAN.																																		
FEB.																																		
MAR.																																		
APR.																																		
MAY																																		
JUNE																																		
JULY																																		
AUG.																																		
SEPT.																																		
OCT.																																		
NOV.																																		
DEC.																																		

Instructions: A separate sheet to be maintained for each child. Each day to be marked to indicate present or absent and kept current on a daily basis.

This sheet to be the basis for preparation of invoice, and available for audit by the State Department of Social Services or its representative.

Proposed Operating Budget
Family Day Care Service

Fiscal Year 197_ to 197_   Serving 50 Family Day Care Homes

EXPENSES   STAFF

I. PERSONNEL	NUMBER FULL-TIME	PART-TIME		MONTHLY AMOUNT	ANNUAL AMOUNT
		NUMBER	WEEKLY HOURS		
A. Central Office					$00,000
Director					
Home-Finders					
Program Aides					
Vocational Counselor					
Clerical					00,000
B. Day Care Homes					
Day Mothers					
C. Consultants					0,000
D. Fringe Benefits					0,000

II. OFFICE EXPENSE

Rent	$00	Telephone & Postage	
Heat	00	Office Equipment & Supplies	
Electricity	00	Insurance	
Maintenance	00		
			0,000

III. DAY CARE HOME EXPENSE

Food:
   (children attending full-time) 200 children @ 00¢ per day per child, including breakfast, lunch & snacks
   School age children attending part-time—100 children @ 0¢ each

Equipment and Plan Materials:
   300 children @ $00 per child per year   0,000

IV. CHILDREN'S HEALTH SERVICES

   Medical Supplies   Emergency Service   0,000

V. INSURANCES	Annual Amount
Fire, Theft & Vandalism for Offices	000
Public Liability for Day Care Homes	000
Social Security (Employer's Share)	000
Unemployment Insurance	000
Workmen's Compensation Insurance	000
Disability Insurance	000
Total Operating Expenses	000,000

Income	
Parents' Fees	000
Public Funds	
Federal:	000,000
Local:	0,000
United Way	0,000
Board of Directors	0,000
Total Income	000,000

appendix C

Agencies and Organizations Concerned with the Early Education of Children*

Alexander Graham Bell Association for the Deaf, Inc., 1537 35th Street, N.W., Washington, D.C. 20007. A private nonprofit organization which works to promote the teaching of speech and lipreading to the deaf with the use of residual hearing. The official journal is *The Volta Review* (nine issues yearly, $12.50). Numerous books and pamphlets are published as well as a newsletter, *Speaking Out,* and a magazine, *World Traveler.* They also house a book lending library for members of the Association and an educational film rental service available to the general public.

American Foundation for the Blind, 15 West 16th Street, New York, New York 10011. A private nonprofit agency which serves as a clearinghouse on all pertinent information about blindness and promotes the development of educational, rehabilitation, and social welfare services for the blind and deaf-blind children and adults. Services include publications in print, large type, recorded and braille forms (limited), the manufacture and sale of special aids and appliances for use by blind people, and recording and manufacture of talking books. Publications include, *AFB Newsletter* (quarterly, free), *New Outlook for the Blind* (monthly, $6, ink, braille, recorded), and *Talking Book Topics* (6 times a year, free to blind persons).

American Association of Elementary-Kindergarten-Nursery Educators (EKNE), NEA, 1201 16th Street, N.W., Washington, D.C. 20036. This affiliate of NEA deals with all the organizations involved in early childhood on national and regional levels. A 1970-71 list of publications, tapes, films, membership information, and a calendar of activities is available through writing EKNE.

Association for Childhood Education International (ACEI), 3615 Wisconsin Avenue, N.W., Washington, D.C. ACEI is an educational organization concerned with the education of young children 2 to 12. It maintains a library service open to the public and also houses nursery and kindergarten materials. Membership is $12.00 yearly with a subscription to the journal *Childhood Education.* Bulletins, portfolios, position papers, and books on early childhood education are available from the Association. Publications available include:

- "Bibliography of Books for Children"
- "Bits and Pieces" (uses for miscellaneous things)
- "Children and T.V."
- "Children's Books for $1.50 or Less"
- "Discipline"
- "A Lap to Sit On—and Much More" (day care aides)

Black Child Development Institute, 1028 Connecticut Avenue, N.W., Suite 514, Washington, D. C. 20036. This Institute which focuses on black child development programs has as its main concern rendering technical assistance to predominantly black day care centers. Available publications include *The Black Child Development Dispatch* (monthly, free).

Child Study Association of America, 9 East 89th Street, New York, New York 10010. A pioneer agency in parent education which for over 80 years has served to strengthen family living through parent group education and counseling programs by training professionals and community aides, and through its research and publications.

---

*Directory of Resources on Early Childhood Education, Lynne Glassman, Council for Exceptional Children Information Center, 1411 South Jefferson Davis Highway, Arlington, Virginia 22202, pp. 13-17.

Child Welfare League of America, 44 East 23rd Street, New York, New York 10010. This organization is involved in all aspects of child welfare—day care service, adoption, and foster family care. *Child Welfare* is the monthly periodical which is a professional journal concerned with the welfare of children—yearly, $6.00; 3 years $15.00; individual issues, $.75.

Day Care and Child Development Council of America, Inc. 1401 "K" Street, N.W., Washington, D.C. The goal of this Council is to promote the development of a locally controlled, publicly supported, universally available child care system through public education, social action, and assistance to local committees, the child, the family, and the community. Annual dues for individuals are $10.00; for families, $15.00; for agencies, $25.00. Publications include:

• *Voice for Children,* published monthly
• *Action for Children,* published six times a year
• *Council Bulletin,* a "hot line" news bulletin, printed as needed to give fast information on important and newsworthy items.

The Council also has a Publications Delivery Service which publishes and distributes at little or no cost pamphlets, brochures, and articles on program development, legislative matters, early childhood education and training, and other vital matters. A listing of these materials is available from the Council.

National Association for the Education of Young Children, 1834 Connecticut Avenue, N.W. Washington, D.C. 20009. This organization maintains a membership of 200 affiliate groups across the country which are involved in setting up new nursery schools.

Major publications dealing with the education of young children

The following periodicals contribute to the literature of young children by focusing entirely or in part on early childhood education.

American Education, U.S. Department of Health, Education, and Welfare, Office of Education. U.S. Government Printing Office, Superintendent of Documents, Washington, D.C. 20402. Ten issues, $9.95.

Children Today, U.S. Department of Health, Education, and Welfare, Children's Bureau. U.S. Government Printing Office, Superintendent of Documents, Washington, D.C. 20402. Bimonthly, $3.90.

Childhood Education, 3615 Wisconsin Avenue, Washington, D.C. 20016. Monthly during the school year, $6.00.

Exceptional Children, The Council for Exceptional Children, 1411 South Jefferson Davis Highway, Suite 900, Arlington, Virginia 22202. Nine issues, $10.00.

The Exceptional Parent, Box 45. Newtonville, Massachusetts 02160. Ten issues, $6.00.

Head Start Newsletter, U.S. Department of Health, Education, and Welfare, Washington, D.C. 20201. Monthly, free.

Today's Education (formerly *NEA Journal),* National Education Association, 1201 16th Street, N.W., Washington, D.C. 20036. Nine issues, $1.05.

Young Children, National Association for the Education of Young Children, 1834 Connecticut Avenue, N.W., Washington, D.C. Six Issues, $5.00.

Department of Health, Education, and Welfare Regional Offices

Region I

Department of Health, Education, and Welfare
Office of Human Development
Office of Child Development
John F. Kennedy Federal Building
Government Center
Boston, Massachusetts 02203
617-223-6867

Region II

Department of Health, Education, and Welfare
Office of Human Development
Office of Child Development
26 Federal Plaza
New York, New York 10007
212-264-4626

Region III

Department of Health, Education, and Welfare
Office of Human Development
Office of Child Development
Post Office Box 12900
Philadelphia, Pennsylvania 19108
215-597-9172

Region IV

Department of Health, Education, and Welfare
Office of Human Development
Office of Child Development
50 Seventh Street, N.E.
Atlanta, Georgia 30323
404-526-5021

Region V

Department of Health, Education, and Welfare
Office of Human Development
Office of Child Development
Room 712—New Post Office Building
433 West Van Buren Street
Chicago, Illinois 60607
312-353-4235

Region VI

Department of Health, Education, and Welfare
Office of Human Development
Office of Child Development
1114 Commerce Street
Dallas, Texas 75202
214-749-3743

Region VII

Department of Health, Education, and Welfare
Office of Human Development
Office of Child Development
Federal Office Building
601 East Twelfth Street
Kansas City, Missouri 64106
816-374-2381

Region VIII

Department of Health, Education, and Welfare
Office of Human Development
Office of Child Development
9017 Federal Office Building
19th and Stout Street
Denver, Colorado 80202
303-837-4284

Region IX

Department of Health, Education, and Welfare
Office of Human Development
Office of Child Development
Federal Office Building
50 Fulton Street
San Francisco, California 94102
415-556-7800

Region X

Department of Health, Education, and Welfare
Office of Human Development
Office of Child Development
Arcade Building
1319 Second Avenue
Seattle, Washington 98101
206-538-0425

★ U.S. GOVERNMENT PRINTING OFFICE: 1973—508–105